Second Man on the Rope

BIOGRAPHY

Ian Mitchell was born in Aberdeen and now lives in Glasgow. He has wandered the Scottish hills for three decades and has also visited the Alps, the Pyrenees and Norway. With Dave Brown he has written two books, *Mountain Days and Bothy Nights* and *A View from the Ridge*, which was joint winner of the 1991 Boardman-Tasker Prize for Mountain Literature.

SECOND MAN ON THE ROPE

MOUNTAIN DAYS WITH DAVIE

IAN MITCHELL

Illustrations by Maggie Ramage

JAMES THIN
THE MERCAT PRESS, EDINBURGH
1992

First published in 1992 by Mercat Press
James Thin, 53 South Bridge, Edinburgh EH1 1YS

© Ian Mitchell 1992
© Illustrations, Maggie Ramage 1992

ISBN 1873644019

Typeset by Polyprint,
48 Pleasance, Edinburgh EH8 9TJ

Printed and bound in Great Britain by
Billing & Sons Limited, Worcester

DEDICATION

This book is dedicated to Davie in the hope that someday he might forgive me for writing it.

DISCLAIMER

Any resemblance in this book to characters living or dead, or to actual events, is not coincidental. It is testimony to the skill of the author.

THANKS

I would like to thank Peter Hodgkiss, who read the manuscript in draft form and made helpful comments. I would also like to thank Joan MacKenzie, who did likewise, and also corrected the Gaelic spelling.

CONTENTS

Preface	1
Rover's Return	3
Lagan Behind	8
A Hourn Escape	15
A Torrid Affair	22
The End of Something	27
Coldsville	33
Cockaleekie	39
Fire and Ice	44
The Ridge and the Midge	48
Special Offer	55
The Ascent of Nymphet Crack	60
Before a Fall	64
Trench Warfare	71
Hohenweg	77
The Young Team	85
Forcan Terrible	91
Rats' Feet on Broken Past	97
Keeping Cuillin Difficulty	102
Crossing the River	111
Crowberry Curfew	117
A Short Walk with Our Publisher	122
Completing: the End of an Auld Sang	128

PREFACE

The following miscellany of tales is offered to readers in the hope that they might enjoy both the incidents of Scottish mountaineering life depicted within, and the portrayal of the main character, Davie, whose name appears on the title page of the collection. Some words by way of a preface may be, however, helpful.

The tales themselves are all based on real incidents. They thus follow the structure of reality, which is anecdotal and episodic, and are not tidied up in any way to provide an artificial dramatic structure. Those who know the hills will know that this is the structure of mountain experience. The tales — which are arranged in roughly chronological order — cover the period of the 1980s, and reflect the social and climbing preoccupations of that decade in which we were brought together, after having had separate developments previously. Behind the tales lies our common philosophy, of Nature not as an escape from or resolution of the problems of life, but as an area for their reproduction. Hopefully, though, this is not expressed too ponderously, in that I see the comedy of the serious, as well as the seriousness of the comic.

Those who know the Scottish hills will also know Davie. Many will know him personally, but most others will know someone like him. For, although in some ways unique, Davie is a typical Scottish character, irascible yet kindhearted, parsimonious yet generous, catholic yet parochial at the same time. Indeed those familiar with mountain literature may recognise antecedents of him in MacSnorrt, from "The Orra Lads' Tale".

> The first ane's name, or so I'm told
> Was John MacSnorrt, and he was bold,
> A tall, camsteerie, ugly chiel,
> Wha's temper was the verra de'il.

I am not claiming for myself the mantle of his timorous pal, Willie:

A little man wha's build was slight,
His shanks were thin, his hands were wee,
An inconspicuous lad was he,*

— though the reader may award his or her own laurels.

Davie is in many ways the quintessence of the 1960s Scottish 'Severe' man, despite the company he now keeps. Aside from the climbing, that type sought the 'total mountain experience' in weekending, bothying and camaraderie. Davie's greatest critique of any mountaineering book — whatever the level of the mountaineering — is 'there's nae people in it; he cannae hae ony pals!'

But today the routes he climbed and — less frequently — climbs, are regarded as easy by the 'E'-men, and his hills covered by Munro-baggers. Both groups have this in common — they tend to be day-outers, and narrow the range of the mountain experience. Davie on the other hand believes in 'keeping the dialectic open' as they used to say in the '60s.

Davie is a real person, with whom I have co-authored two books, and to whom this third is dedicated, with affection, for all the tight ropes, and as a contribution to the struggle against cultural entropy. I trust it does not make him regret the time he said, when I complained I was running out of ideas for mountain literature, 'well, ye can write aboot me!'

This book is a celebration of a man, of — I hope — a friendship, and of the Scottish hills which were the crucible for that friendship.

---

* The full text of "The Orra Lads' Tale" is printed in *A Century of Scottish Mountaineering* (S.M.T.), pp 107-8.

ROVER'S RETURN

It was the first time I had been away with Davie. After several unsuccessful starts, I seemed to have found someone in Glasgow whose passion for the hills matched mine. But could I pass muster with my new companion? I already knew him as an associate of the fearful Creag Dhu; he had climbed with many of the best men of his generation; he had been to the Himalayas, the Alps and the Rockies. A curriculum vitae which cast my own modest achievements in a very large shadow — as he had already pointed out to me. More than once.

'Ye must realise,' he said, 'that I've been tae yer secret howff before. This is no the first time.'

I already knew Davie well enough to realise that Big Euan and myself were about to hear the full, unexpurgated version of his first visit to the hidey hole that I had not revisited during my decade's exile in Glasgow. I was glad Davie knew of it. It relieved me of the responsibility of wondering whether I was breaking the obscure and convoluted rules governing Slugain Howff's secrecy, by taking him to it. And Davie himself could be regarded as taking Big Euan.

'It was Sandy that took me. An Aberdonian. He'd been a gamie on the estate o' Invercauld. He was a queer bugger, typical Aberdonian,' he said, looking at me. 'Really mean.'

I knew I would have to buy the drinks at the Fife Arms in Braemar, to avoid being tarred with the same brush.

'He used tae tak wan spoon o' sugar at haim, and two if he was visiting yer hoose.'

'Maybe he was takkin a lane o' ye Davie?' I suggested.

'No, no,' he came back, irked at the suggestion that his perspicacity could be so wanting. 'He used tae leave his wife in the car tae save money when he went tae the pub. I saw her sittin there when I went oot.'

This did seem difficult to gainsay, so I tried to change the topic.

3

'Tell us aboot the trip tae the howff.'

'Well, we met some o' his auld workmates in the pub, and we got well oiled; ye should hae seen them, strappin lads wi Glenmorangie tartan faces. So it wis late when we got tae the howff, aifter gettin chucked oot at midnight, and the lang walk. And maybe we were a bit noisy comin in and frying up the square sassidges, and finishing oor cairry-oot. But that wis nae excuse for the lot that wis there already for jist glowerin at us and refusing tae be friendly, like. Ye know me, I'm aye prepared tae be accommodating and welcoming.'

I knew Davie, or was getting to know him. Knew that behind that body language that might have made the unknowing think they were about to be challenged to a 'fair go', lurked a genuinely tender and sensitive soul, seeking communion. I suggested that possibly, in the wee sma oors, and also the worse for drink, his desire to make a contribution to the *Weltgemeinschaft* might not have been apparent to an innocent onlooker.

'Ah, bit wait,' he cried, obviously with his trump card to come. 'In the morning we wernae noisy. But that crowd o' tight-arsed Aberdonians just got up and left, withoot a word!'

He mentioned names; some I knew, others only by repute. I had lost contact with the Aberdeen scene, but felt somehow still obliged to defend them.

'Maybe they were gyan onywye?'

No, he rejected this; it was just the pure ill-nature and parochialism of warped east-coasters, faced with friendly men of the west.

'I wouldnae be sae polite now, if I got yon kind o' reception again,' muttered Davie, working himself up into a street-fighting posture and frame of mind in the driver's seat. But he soon faced a real conflict, from another and unexpected quarter.

We drove past the NO ENTRY sign at the Invercauld gates, took the back road past the lodge, and parked at a locked gate a couple of miles on. I suggested haste to avoid detection, but Euan and Davie were dilatory in packing up to go. And we paid the price. Without looking, I could picture what was coming up behind us, from the heavy scrunch on the track. The gamie stood there, fearsome in tweed and windburn, glowering at us. We waited for him to speak.

'Aye, and fit wid you loons be daein wi that car. Can ye no read? Did ye get permission tae come up here?'

A trick question, trying to trap us.

'Naw, fair doose. We didnae,' said Davie.

'And far wid yeeze be gyan?' he asked.

I decided to see if I could talk us out of a humiliating drive back, and walk back up from the road.

'We're gyan tae the howff, I've nae been there for ten year, used tae ging there a' the time. Kent the lads that built it' (that was stretching it a bit, but what the hell). 'We used tae be able tae drive up richt tae the gate . . .'

He was obviously a bit mollified by the reference to the howff. By a curious paradox, though the Invercauld gamies were zealously proprietorial, the select users of the howff were tolerated and its existence allowed to go unchecked.

'And it was Sandy that used to work here, that took me tae the howff,' ventured Davie.

'Sandy, ye ken Sandy?' But then he stiffened. 'But there's oer much vandalism noo, we cannae let ye leave the car here.'

'Listen,' I ventured, 'dae we look like vandals? And if onything happens, ye've got the car here.'

Davie looked as if he was about to protest at his four wheels being used as ransom, when the gamie indicated that he was won over.

'A' richt, a' richt. Hide it in the wid doon by.' He pointed to some trees where a side track led. We thanked him profusely, and cached the vehicle.

'Ye see Davie,' I commented, 'ye've jist tae ken foo tae treat east coasters.'

But I was struck for words when he replied, 'Aye, it wis me mentioning Sandy that won him oer.'

After a walk in the fine evening light, we were soon entering the tiny door of the howff — the 'secret howff' of Beinn a' Bhuird where I had spent many weekends a decade previously. I had come back to Slugain Howff for nostalgia. Davie and Euan had come to climb; so there was a divergence the next day, when we emerged from the dwarf's house, built into its sheltering rock, quite obscured from chance gaze.

'C'mon,' encouraged Davie, 'come wi us tae Garbh Choire. Ye'll manage Squareface, and we've two ropes.'

Davie's optimism was based on my modest clutch of Cairngorm routes, dating from over a decade previously. Lack of partners and loss of interest had led to no additions since then.

'I'll come wi ye, but I'll nae climb. I'll ging on tae Beinn a' Chaorainn and see ye back at the Howff.'

'Beinn a' Chaorainn! I used tae tak the Tufties fae Glenmore Lodge tae yon daft hill. That's no fit for a real man's outing.'

I had to suffer a little more baiting before my spectator's role was accepted. We trudged the long miles past Clach a' Chleirich and on to Garbh Choire, descending to the foot of the Sneck, and then on to Mitre Ridge, where the pair took their stance at the bottom of the Crofton-Cumming route. Once more I rejected participation, moving instead up the hill to watch their progress up the Ridge. That was the day I decided to purchase a camera, cursing the lost photo opportunities.

The Mitre Ridge, as those who have seen it will be aware, is a magnificent sweep of rock, 650 feet high, crowned by jaggy towers. The west wall is virtually vertical, and on it the classic they had chosen was described as 'continuously difficult and exposed'. I watched as Euan led off and climbed to a shelf, and then over a hanging flake to the first belay, where he was silhouetted above the black rock against the blue sky. I had never climbed that confidently, I thought. Davie followed, in a more muscular style, and led through; then traversed to the second belay, where he appeared to be standing on air. I moved up the hill, taking myself farther from them, to follow. I lost them occasionally as they dipped between the Ridge and its subsidiary, but always they would reappear against the fine sky, moving very quickly. They were soon standing together on a large platform near the top of the Mitre. Then one of them (I was too far to discern whom) moved onto what seemed a holdless wall, and gained the summit.

We met at the north top for lunch; they were exultant.

'Yon Bell's variation. That's something,' enthused Davie, adding, 'Ye missed yersel there. Squareface is still an option, if ye want?'

Tempted, I declined, leaving them to descend again while I crossed the barren boulder fields of Beinn a' Bhuird, and then bounced across the springy, easy turf of the Moine Bhealaidh to my top; where I dozed in the thin sunlight, dreaming, watching the deer, listening to the black cock calling.

Dreaming.

In the howff, when I arrived back, a Squareface obituary was going on. I had passed Coire na Ciche on the return, and looked, tried to remember what it was I had done there. Not a great deal, and most of the time I had been traumatised. The Sickle sounded familiar . . .

'Exposed and steep, but a bit short,' Euan was saying. 'And quite easy. Not a patch on Crofton-Cumming.'

'Aye,' Davie looked up, 'Ye'd hae managed it nae bother. We'll get ye back on the rock yet!'

'Aye, mebbe,' I smiled.

'And it's important tae keep daein these fine auld routes. The modren thinking is dismissive, looking for wee daft short impossible climbs in quarries and things. The traditions must be kept up!'

'But that's just fit Sandy was daeing wi the sugar, Davie,' I ventured.

'Eh? Ye're bletherin, man. But that reminds me, we'd better get doon quick the morra. Yon gamie might nick wir petrol cap or something. I widnae pit it past an Aberdonian tae nick yer windscreen wipers.'

So I had to atone for all the real and imaginary sins of my compatriots by buying the drink on the way home as well.

LAGAN BEHIND

And Davie did get me back on the rocks before too long. I was fortunate; he was getting to that stage where he was running out of partners, and had to make do with what was on offer. His old Creag Dhu pals had dispersed, and he was still without acolytes.

I had been trudging through Knoydart, in the rain. From Glen Dessary I had taken the old hill track to Sourlies, hoping it would clear. Then I had crossed the unseen hills to Inverie and given up. Davie and the Young Doctor were at Sligachan, so I decided to join them, hoping my luck and the weather would change. A hop on the wee boat to Mallaig, a skip on the ferry to Armadale, and a jump on the bus to Sligachan, and I was looking for Davie's tent.

These were the last days of free camping at Sligachan, before boulders were rolled and ground dug up to force use of the Hotel's camp site. Free camping at Glen Brittle had already gone, much to Davie's chagrin. He approached the philosophical issue of access from an economic, rather than a moral standpoint.

'Thirty bob tae pit up yer tent, it's daylight robbery!'

I found it. They were not there, so I headed for the bar.

They had had a good day; some route down by the Cioch, and they were celebrating. Davie commented: 'There's a fine auld gentlemen's route near by, that naebody does now, on the next buttress. Steeple and Barlow's Direct Route. And they're rights o' way, these auld routes. If naebody uses them, they get closed.'

He paused, and fixed me steely eyed.

'We're for it the morra. Ye can coont yersel in, if ye like.'

I realised it was more of an instruction than a question. On it could depend my occupation of a corner of his tent the next day.

We drove down to Brittle in reassuringly bad weather. Mist

pressed on the roof of the car, and we could see little as we trudged up through freezing precipitation into Coire Lagan. We passed below the Cioch, invisible above, to the foot of the Eastern Buttress. Davie was downcast as he stared at the dripping rocks. The Young Doctor suggested making the most of it, and having a stroll to the top of Sgurr Sgumain, just to stretch the legs. With much muttering and cursing we stumbled up the Sgumain stoneshoot in the enveloping mist, gaining the Bealach Coire a' Ghrunnda where we stalled for an early lunch. Silently.

I have seen it again, but never like that. One minute there was a blank sheet of mist. Then suddenly an uplift warm breeze tugged at it, and subsided. Then it whipped up again, and tore some fleeting rents. Minutes later we were sitting marooned by mist on one of an archipelago of peaks. A Cuillin atoll floated above Coire Lagan filled with a white evanescent sea of cloud. Sgurr Alasdair, Sgurr Mhic Choinnich, Sgurr Dearg, islands in the cloud-sea. No one had spoken while this happened. My thoughts turned to a celestial boat, which one could sail to the peaks in turn.

Then Davie broke the silence.

'It's still misty below, and it'll still be cauld and weet. What aboot the Coire Lagan round? The passes are clagged in, but the peaks are clear, and should dry oot. We can get a good day after a'.'

A hurried packing preceded continuation. Soon we were over Sgumain, and descended to the Bad Step of Sgurr Alasdair. We were in the half-mist again, and to me it looked intimidating. I took courage and stated, 'I'd like a rope for this'.

While Davie muttered, the Young Doctor shot off and disappeared, his umbilical cord hanging behind him and seeming to have a life of its own. After he had wrapped the rope twice round the mountain he called on me to follow. The next step required even greater courage on my part than asking for the rope.

'Davie, I've forgotten hoo tae tie knots.'

A brief explosion of amazement gave way to a weary resignation.

'Tae think! Tae think! I've clumb wi some o' the best men o' my generation. Cunningham, Higgins and the like. And tae think . . . Noo listen. The wee rabbit comes oot o' the hole, and goes behind the tree. . . .'

He showed me, accompanied by the animal metaphor. I was

not sure if I had done it right, but was afraid to ask for a check, and shot off upwards.

On reaching Sgurr Alasdair, it cleared farther. Below us we could see Loch Coire a' Ghrunnda, and ahead of us the tide of the mist had gone out, and connected the archipelago ahead into a long peninsula. The rock was drying out swiftly. We scrambled quickly to the bealach below Sgurr Mhic Choinnich. Here Davie saved me the embarrassment of asking again by uncoiling the rope below King's Chimney.

'There's still a lot of watter in it. We'll use the rope, jist in case.'

Again the Young Doctor was sent on ahead, while Davie had a wee snooze. I followed up the chimney, then worked out of it by a steep slab past an overhang. Soon we were on top of the tiny summit, then working our way down the narrow arete to the foot of An Stac. But much as I had enjoyed my day's scrambling, I had had enough by the time we reached the Pinnacle of Sgurr Dearg. So I rested and took photographs of Davie and the Doctor silhouetted against the monolith, while I ate the last of my food.

Returning, Davie exulted, 'That was a great day. Victory snatched fae the jaws o' defeat. And ye've felt the rugosities o' the rock again!'

It was late, and a long time since we had eaten. So we were ravenous when we entered the bar. We envisaged a long night ahead, eating, drinking and watching the World Cup semi-finals. The game had already started and France were beating West Germany 3-1 when we ordered our pints, and the alcohol hit empty stomachs. The barman came back and I caught his attention, asking for the menu. He was about to speak, when he looked and saw my companions. Davie was looking strangely sheepish, avoiding the barman's eyes.

'The food's off,' the barman said, and walked away.

I was stunned.

'Fit dae ye mak o' that, Davie?'

'I had a run in wi' him a few years ago. I stole his lassie at a dance. He's never forgiven me. Just let it gae bye.'

'Let it gae bye! I'm tae starve jist because you couldnae keep yer willie under control twenty year ago! Ye must be jokin!'

I was ready to do battle, with whom I was not sure. But Davie and the Doctor calmed me down, and we ate nuts and crisps, while West Germany equalised, and then went on to win. As we waltzed back unsteadily to the tent at midnight, Davie said, 'aye, ye'd be getting intae awful trouble, withoot me tae look aifter ye.'

To what was he referring?

When we got back to try at Direct Route again, there were no free camp sites anywhere; so we went to Brittle, being the nearest. It was eight years later and we were with the Young Team. As they unloaded their luminous lycra strips, they were stunned to see Davie, intent on his comfort, removing both a folding chair and a camp bed from his car.

'Nae point in being uncomfortable,' he ventured.

Benny and Kenny were intent on Cioch West, with possibly Integrity to follow (or at least, Benny was). So we left them at the traffic jam below the Cioch and headed on to the foot of Direct Route on the neighbouring buttress, where Davie assured us we would be alone.

'First done in 1912 . . .' he read from his guidebook.

'Has it been deen since?' I asked.

He ignored me, and continued, 'this is the kind o' route description I like, "The route follows the most obvious line to the top". Nane o' yer instructions whar tae pit yer left tae, and hoo mony inches between hauds.'

We stumbled about a bit, looking for the start. Bobby was with us, shivering in his T-shirt and trainer bottoms, impatient. Davie shook his head.

'Ye're no dressed for the occasion. Ye'd think ye were aff tae the Whangie, in that gear!'

But soon he was leading off, over a long, slanting, steepish slab, to disappear round a corner. We followed over an easyish pitch, which was strenuous enough to get muscles and adrenalin working. At a narrow platform, we looked vertically down into the Sgumain stoneshoot. While Bobby and I searched the Cioch face for the two others, Davie moved over a steep sloping slab which looked decidedly holdless, and reached the foot of a steep chimney.

We had time to admire the view, as Davie gave us a running commentary on his plight. The chimney was still wet and slippy, and he was struggling to reach the top and pull out. But eventually he did so, muttering, 'V.Diff. V.Diff? That's mair nor V.Diff.'

In vibrams I found the slab much more problematic, but with a longer reach, and the security of a top rope, climbed the

chimney without a hitch. Bobby followed behind as usual: uncomplaining and wordless, like a wee puppy on a lead.

A series of easier pitches followed, and we thought we must be up. But then the ground levelled away, before rising finally to the crux: a vertical wall. We had a little break for sustenance and then Davie spidered up the wall, to announce we were at the top. I found it murder; wee holds my boot toes would not go into, and cracks that made my fingers feel like pounds of sausages. I went half way up, then down. Did the same again. I could not see Davie, but he was uttering his usual words of encouragement, something about the dubious sexual morals of my mother and wife. But then I thought: he can't see me either, if I can't see him.

I moved back up to the point I had previously gained, and then reached for the krab attaching the rope to the sling. It seemed firm, so I pulled up, and then slipped my feet into the sling as I passed.

'Naething tae it, ance ye got the idea,' I announced on arrival. He scowled.

'Get Bobby up here quick, it's gonna rain.'

I looked at the sky, and sure enough, it had turned steely bluegrey, and a gusty wind rose. Bobby benefitted from my silent example, and reached the top in due course.

The heavens opened. Hailstones stotted down. It was summer, after all. Bobby was coiling the rope, in payment for his day out, while Dave and I donned layers of warm and protective clothing. Bobby meanwhile was almost naked, apart from the rope which he had coiled and slung over his shoulder. He was shivering, teeth chittering, and turning a funny colour. We gave him what we had to give: a spare bunnet and a pair of gloves, a lightweight jacket. And a lexicon of curses and epithets, conveying precious information as to the future apparel he might consider suitable for the Cuillin. We descended to Glen Brittle in the hail and rain.

I later discovered that Murray said of this route:

'The most charming route in Skye. None of us knows a better. . . . decidedly harder then the route's official classification. I cannot recall enjoying a Cuillin climb more . . .' (*Undiscovered Scotland*).

When I read this out to Davie, he assumed I was trying to argue that there was no need for me to do any of the others . . .

Kenny and Benny? Well, they got to the crux of Cioch West, and Kenny refused to go further. So Benny had to reverse the crux, and then they climbed back down, apologising, through the dozens of people who were on their way up. Benny cursed him down, cursed him to the tent, cursed him home. Cursed him drunk, and cursed him sober. It was the end of Kenny's brilliant climbing career.

'Ye should hae come wi' us,' said Davie. 'Oors wis the better route, onywye. Yon Cioch West is overrated.'

A HOURN ESCAPE

It should not have been snowing, it was too early. In fact it was not snowing when we left, only drizzling the usual November drizzle. Why did we always seem to get going away for bothy weekends in November? To sit disappointed round a flickering fire, spurning the rain-clagged hills, and wishing the snow would come. Definitely a case for the sacking of the Stobcross Gentlemen's Climbing Club Secretary: only that was me.

'The Young Doctors are coming as weel,' announced Davie, as we loaded the car, 'but they'll be later than us. It's always good to have medical men on an expedition. Mind you, wi' the bold young Lochinvar and Doctor Death, I'm no sure that'll be much comfort.'

As most journeys went, it was uneventful; and by the time the road end at Kinlochhourn was gained the rain had stopped, and the sky cleared, to reveal the heavens festooned with stars, but no moon. My limited astronomy tried to explain why you could have stars, but no moon, and gave up in confusion. The sky was blueblack, the mountains of Loch Hourn inkblack, and the loch itself silverblack. Further along the loch we could see the lights of Arnisdale, twinkling like some fallen-to-earth stars. We started along the old military road, built to pacify the Jacobites and the brigands like Coll of Barrisdale who pillaged far and wide. Past the ruins of a pier, one built possibly to serve the herring fishing in Loch Hourn a century ago. Then the loch was black in daytime: black with the fleets of fishing vessels berthed in it. As I walked, looking at the tones of black, I thought I understood at last the meaning of 'the shades of night'.

Much of the ground underfoot still bore the remains of the old military road, and we sped along, invigorated by the cold night air and the views ahead. But the road followed the principles of all such, from the Romans to Wade; it went straight. Not contouring round high hills and headlands, but over them; up and down, up and down we peched with heavy packs, till, sweating profusely, we reached the sands of Barrisdale Bay. Another mile or so, past the House, and we got to the bothy itself.

This trip was just before Knoydart became an official wilderness and therefore much visited, and before the Barrisdale bothy was gentrified. The building retained its air of having been, probably, an estate workers' habitation, and was in a state of mild disrepair. But it had a gas range, which heated the water, and a bath, scabby perhaps, but connected to the water system. Davie was reading the notice on the wall to occupants. 'It says here it's a pound each night, up to four in the party, and ten bob if there's mair than four.'

I could see him calculating.

'That means it's cheaper for five, than for four. I vote we add another member to our party, and split the difference.'

As well as indicating Davie's parsimony, this sally indicated his verbal conservatism. Fifty pence was still ten bob, the radio was still the wireless, and strikers were still centre-forwards.

The weather was changing, and by the time the Young Doctors arrived, the rain was pelting down; they entered, cold and dripping, to the hut, where we were getting our money's worth of gas, toasting by the fire. After a brief exchange of pleasantries, we bedded hoping for better weather the next day. One can hope. Like the man who built the Station Hotel at Rhynie. When it was pointed out to him that Rhynie did not have a railway, he commented, 'Aye, but I wis aye hopin.' Good weather in Scotland is a bit like the Rhynie railway.

But next day the train of good weather had not arrived. It was lashing down in the famous Knoydart buckets, set fair to beat the 11 inches in a day record the region holds for the U.K. Thick cloud rolled over the colourless landscape. The Young Doctors made their first gambit for a retreat, arguing for an exit and home. Davie was appalled.

'A' this modern gear, these lycra babygrows ye wear, has corroded yer moral fibre. Ye gie the hill a chance, then ye see. Gae haim, I never heard the like!'

This stunned them into silence, and into donning the various accoutrements of which Davie disapproved, and we got them out, heading for Ladhar Bheinn. Crossing the first river was no problem, there was a bridge. Crossing the second was, though it was only a few feet wide, since there was no bridge, and the water was about six feet deep. The sacks were thrown over, and then a big loup joined their owners with them.

'It's clearing,' said Davie, looking at the rolling cloud and vertical columns of rain, legions of them on a silent march. So we took the good stalkers' path round into the corrie, and headed up the burn. Across the glen lay the ridge leading towards the summit of our mountain. As we headed into the corrie, the wind hit us; not any hurricane, but enough to add markedly to the discomfort of the driving rain. Then we had our first casualty; young Lochinvar doubled up in agony. Later we discovered it was the skimpy underpants, fashionable in those pre-boxer-short days, that were restricting his circulation.

'Oh, I'm in agony, I can't go on. Go without me.'

'Whit the f—— is the matter wi' ye?'

'I don't know.'

'Don't know, and ye're a bloody doctor! I hope I don't wake up on an operating table wi' you stauning oer me.'

We carried on without him for a few hundred yards, then the other one started complaining. He at least was honest.

'This is murder. I'm going back.'

And he headed off after his professional companion.

We carried on to the burn, raging in torrents down the glen, and crossed it with difficulty, carrying on till we reached the lower part of the ridge leading to the summit. In the mist and rain it looked very far away. On the ridge the wind was screeching, and we sheltered behind some rocks. Davie looked thoughtful.

'I'm worried aboot yon rivers,' he finally announced. 'I was wance in Knoydart wi' Conn Higgins, and we'd tae climb the mountain again to get across the river we crossed in the morning. This rain is getting worse. We've gien the hill its chance, let's gae back.'

I ventured resistance. I'd just become a daddy, and in some obscure way this had awakened an interest in Munro bagging in me: this would be my 100th Munro. I tried to explain to Davie about the emergence of new life, leading to awareness of death, and the desire to leave a mark. If not of great new routes, at least that of being no 481 on the SMC list of Munroists. I was getting quite carried away on the theme, when an ever more bewildered looking Davie broke in with, 'aye, weel a daddy should be mair interested in getting back tae his wean in wan piece, than risking life and limb on a day like the day. If we dinnae get back soon ye'll maybe no be a daddy for lang.'

He started off, and I followed, half willingly, half un-willingly.

The burn we had crossed quarter of an hour ago was much wider, and we slithered from half sunken boulder to boulder. We were sodden.

'Maybe yon Goretex wouldnae be such a bad idea,' muttered a drookit Davie. 'But it's the price! Ye'd hae tae extend yer mortgage tae buy wan!'

We skirted round the stalkers' path and descended to Barrisdale Bay and the first crossing. It was still only about six feet deep, but was now about ten feet wide, quite unjumpable. We went downstream: no good. We went upstream a mile or more till the burn narrowed to about five feet, and jumped, grabbing tussocks of grass and pulling up on the other side.

'In anither hour, that'll be impassable,' one of us said and the other agreed. The next river had the bridge, so our worries lessened. But the wind did not, and it was blowing straight down the glen, and gusting. Bowling us over now. The bridge had a handrail, a broken one, with a gap of about four feet through which the wind snarled, and below which the water seemed to boil in fury. It was undignified, but there was only one thing for it. Flattened on stomachs, we slithered across the bridge, for fear of being blown through the gap.

At the bothy the medical men had the fire blazing.

'What kept you? Get to the top?'

We scowled, stripped into dry clothes and made our meal. It was still quite early in the day, and after eating I noticed that the water was scalding. I would clean that manky old bath out, and have a bath. That would be a tale to tell! So I got a rag and a bit of soap and scoured away, proudly surveying my work and contemplating my luxurious indulgence to come. But back in the kitchen, it was clear there had been a discussion in my absence. The young men were for leaving that day, and Davie was swithering.

'I dinna like leaving early, but look oot there.'

I looked. It was beginning to sleet. I followed his thoughts; tomorrow we might not be able to fight our way out of Loch Hourn, and there would be no snowplough round on a Sunday.

'But I'm ready for my bath!' I protested weakly. My desire for cleanliness was an insufficient argument to keep them there, and forbye, it was Davie's car we were in, an old 2CV whose powers of endurance in arctic conditions were untested. It was decided to go. Back along that knackering military road, burdened by defeat and disappointment, in the slithering sleet, fording mad roaring burns. I could see it all only too well as I got back into wet clothes, keeping the dry ones for the journey home in the car.

Never can seven miles have been traversed in such sullen silence. Not a word was spoken by the band that retreated from Barrisdale till Kinlochhourn was reached. By this time it was snowing in earnest, though it was still slush by the roadside. The hills were white, and it occurred to me that higher up, towards Tomdoun, the snow would be dry, lying. The Young Doctors were sent off first in a real car, to make tracks the 2CV could follow. The Cortina took the z-bends out of Kinlochhourn with only a little slithering, but the 2CV was all over the place, and kept stalling. While Davie removed the snow that was getting into the electrics under the bonnet, I uncovered piles of road grit, and scattered it with my hands on the bends of the road. I walked a few yards, and the 2CV made a few yards more with only one occupant. Finally, with the help of the Doctors and myself pushing, Davie steered it to the top of the last bend. Just in time; the snow was falling like a blanket now, and it was every man for himself as the medical men abandoned us, their lights vanishing in the blizzard.

I had never believed Davie all the times he had told me what a wonderful driver he was, but after that day, there was no doubting it. At first we could make out and follow the Cortina tracks; but soon it was a total white-out, and the road could not be seen. Even after the windscreen wiper, which clogged continually with snow, was unblocked by one hand as he drove with the other, we could not see the road.

'But I can feel it,' reassured Davie, as he drove on automatic pilot, inching forward, sensing the road edges with the wheels. Every now and then he got out to clear the engine of the snow build-up which stalled it. If a passing-place loomed out of the wilderness, I searched for grit and scattered it with my hands. This was more as an offering to the gods than anything else. I had no hope of being able to battle out. We would have to spend the night in the car, possibly after it had gone off the road. It had been a long time since we had seen the vanishing lights of the Cortina.

Dazzling, a bright yellow glare burst through the curtain of white; we shielded our eyes, and swerved as we saw the snowplough. Inside were two of the most astonished faces I had ever seen looking down on us. They had cleared and gritted the road this far, and were garaging their powerful beast, unable to go further. We were near Tomdoun, we were

out. It had taken us six hours to come the eleven miles from Kinlochhourn. For a while neither of us spoke, in the dark that was suddenly sheltering, rather than threatening.

We drove down the road, leaving the snow behind, but still carrying the trauma of the fight out.

'This calls for pints and haufs at Inverarnan,' announced the driver, and towards that hostelry we headed without further incident. We crossed the porch, passed the stuffed animals and suits of armour gathering dust, and into the pub where a hearty blaze roared. The barman informed us that the Auld Crowd were there. Where? Just follow the singing. We walked into the policies and heard sounds of revelry from under the trees. Saw smoke billowing through the leafless branches to the sky. Avoiding the sheep shit which covered the ground we headed towards the flames.

There were about a dozen of them. They had met to take one of the Purvis brothers, who had multiple sclerosis, up Ben Dorain in a helicopter, but bad weather had cancelled that plan. Making the best of it, they were singing and dancing round the fire.

Wee Onie sang Bob Dylan and Rabbie Burns.

An English fella recited one of those doggerel poems about a lion eating a wee boy at the zoo.

Hector did a Maori dance, complete with facial and bum gestures.

We drank and chatted to them amongst the sheep shit.

Back in the car, Davie asked, 'did I ever tell you the story about that crowd, taking one o' their pals across the Falloch mouth tae Doune Byre? He was pretty bad, a colostomy case, and the boat was overloaded, wi' people and drink. Of course it capsized. Purvis nearly died o' hyopothermia and needed the kiss o' life. The colostomy case sank, but his bag floated on top o' the watter, away downstream. That's what let them rescue him, otherwise he was a gonner. They eventually got to Doune and dried out. But the queerest thing was next day, they go back for the drink. Hector gets weights tied tae his legs, and dives for it tae the bottom o' the river. And gets it.'

He mused for a while.

'Aye, that crowd dinna gae haim when it's raining.'

A TORRID AFFAIR

An uneventful trip? You want an uneventful trip? Well now, I can't really think of any . . . apart from the one I nearly got killed on.

I almost did not go at all. I had just become a daddy, and it was proving a bit much for me. And then the weather was bad when Davie and the others set off, and when they arrived. He had phoned from the Damp Ben bar, looking out through the plate-glass wall at the wilderness of Beinn Damh in the rain. He encouraged me to come, saying that the forecast was good.

So I loaded up the beat-up old banger of a Chevette that I had held on to, hoping it would become a cult car and the price start going up, and headed north and west the next day. And what a day: improving as it went from brilliant to almost beyond belief. As the sun went down the shadows lengthened, gouging out the recesses of the hills, and sharpening and raising their summits. The light was opalescent, and then, heading down to Loch Maree, it turned ultramarine, an ethereal evanescence above Beinn Lair. I stopped and took a photograph to prove that I was not dreaming.

I had not been down that road for years, forgotten it. Beinn Eighe glistened in quartzite diamante in the sun, then Liatach glowed gold like a great furnace. By Loch Torridon I stopped to admire the sun setting behind Beinn Alligin, and burnishing the oily sea. I was in no hurry to get to the pub on such a night.

Then I saw him coming towards me, on the wrong side of the road. Unworried, I waited for the Land Rover to pull over. It hurtled nearer. Swerved across the road and back. I saw the driver, slumped over the wheel and oblivious. I calculated he would hit me, and I had no time to get out of the car. In a panic, I jammed down the horn. The driver jerked up, tore at the wheel, swerved and missed me, swerved again as if about to leave the road, righted up, decelerated, and carried on.

In the pub I saw Davie, Mr 10% and some others, and half heard as they told me of their great day on the sun-kissed rock of the Cioch Nose. I told them of my recent escapade, and after a hush Davie said, 'that's whit I tell the wife. The maist dangerous thing is the driving. Yer safer on the rocks. That reminds me, I've tae phone.'

We downed a couple of pints while Davie phoned his loved one, coming back frequently to get more change and returning to the phone with a worried look. Someone ventured, with a smile, 'tellin yer loved wan aboot yer great deeds on the rocks, Davie?' and got a foul look in reply.

'We're back at the river, doon in the trees. Didnae fancy the camp site,' he told me, as we went for the cars. 'Whaur we aye used tae go.'

'We used tae doss in the S.M.C. stable at the Ling Hut,' I mused. 'But they've locked it and done it up. Market forces rules, noo.'

His 'we' and my 'we' were different 'we's', at that time.

Next day it was Coire McFearchar of Beinn Eighe. The long walk in between Liatach and Beinn Eighe, between sandstone and quartzite, and round past the crashed aeroplane, to the loch below the shattered buttresses. I was uninterested in anything but Sail Liath, a bit like climbing a sandhill in a desert, and left the others to their climbs.

We met again back at the camp, glistening with sweat and aching with exertion, and fell into a deep pool for a swim. The water was shockingly cold, and afterwards 10% started shivering, chittering. Inside a sleeping bag he went, inside him hot soup went, and he gradually recovered. Davie looked at the miserable figure.

'Aye, an yer wife is probably like mine; thinks I come awa tae enjoy masel.'

We did not fancy the pub on such a glorious night, so Davie and I drove to Applecross.

'We'll see the sunset fae the Beedlum Bo,' he said.

My car was falling to bits (Davie's was with his wife). The exhaust had already come half off at the camp and the thing was losing oil as well. But we clattered up to the top of the pass, on the only interesting road left in Britain, and watched from it. Watched the cairns come alive, figures in the falling light. Watched the islands out to sea — Raasay there, slither like a crocodile into the water. There were two colours only: black and red. We watched, watched for a long time.

Coming down the pass in the dark was quite tricky. The Chevette's lights were none too good either. Then Davie said, 'the oil light is on.'

Sure enough, it was. We clattered round in the darkness to Kishorn, where we found a garage owner willing to open up. He filled up, not from a drum, but from wee half-pint cans of oil. I noticed he was an Aberdonian, and putting on my best brogue, ventured to ask, 'foo muckle will this be costin me?'

'Och, dinna worry aboot that the noo,' was the reassuring reply.

He poured and poured, and then charged me about four times the daytime rate.

'Aye, market forces are gettin even tae Aberdonians noo,' chuckled Davie.

I should have put him out, or driven away while I waited for him outside the telephone box. And waited.

'Torrid passion by phone?' I asked, when he returned. He sank into the passenger seat.

'Naw, jist the cat's indigestion,' he sighed.

Next day was again torrid, and those with minds on rocks decided on Fuar Tholl. I went along for the ride, deciding I would walk over via Beinn Liath Mhor to the Ling Hut. So round we went, crossed the railway, and walked up the glen. I met no one on my walk, sailed over the hill and came down by the burn to the Ling. I looked at the converted byre where I had slept a few times in the days when the meagre impost for staying in the luxurious S.M.C. hut appeared exorbitant to me.

My friends started to climb their face, but were attacked by an eagle, who did not approve of their intentions. So they abseiled off. This caused some problems when 10% claimed that 90% of all abseil accidents were caused by not knotting the end of the rope, in case you had to hang on if the rope was too short. In testing this theory, they nearly fell off. It was wet anyway, they said, and looked awfully hard. I pointed out that Fuar Tholl was really a north-easters' crag.

It was a lovely wee camp site, in the trees by the deep pool at the river's bend. Saint Paul had removed a wee divot, and we lit a fire there in the gloaming. We chatted, waiting for a bile, and again forwent the pub. Earl Grey it was. Davie was slightly suspicious.

'In my young days drinking this would hae led tae aspersions being cast on yer manliness.'

25

We discussed medical ethics. Paul had just become a doctor: you could tell by the big shiny car beside my wreck. Davie told him to beware of women, now he was earning.

'And dinna get a flat. I was safe, till I got a flat, and then I couldnae keep them awa.'

We discussed legal ethics, and 10% claimed that 11% of all Americans were lawyers. Davie suggested he had sunstroke and that this was also the root of his absurd ideas about abseiling.

We discussed the hill, and what was behind this activity of ours. We had had a few delightful and unspectacular days, pursuing an activity that brought no profit and no applause. What then, was the meaning behind it all? Self-realisation, communion with nature . . .

'Whit ye see is what ye get. The experience is the experience, there's naething hidden behind it.'

I cannot remember if I said it, or if Davie did, but I remember it disappointed some of the others. For by that time we had both realised it was the only philosophy that kept you going. If you look for something that is not there, you give up on discovering so.

We bedded down when only the embers were left.

Then we went home. I to my two-month-old son, who seemed to know who I was, which was more than I did at that time. We put Paul's divot back, and watered it, before we left.

And that is about as uneventful as I can get.

THE END OF SOMETHING

'A great place tae take a young lady,' Davie was informing me. 'Very romantic down by the loch, and cozy in the bothy.'

We were by now heaving up the incline to the moor. Before us in the sunshine rose the slope of An Teallach. It appeared I was in for a chapter from his sexual odyssey. Appearances were, this time, undeceptive.

'The first time I came here it was wi' a lassie; very nice she was, a' the bits and bobs in the right places, know whit I mean? We'd done An Teallach, she was excited and frightened, kept swooning intae my manly arms, and then down by the loch we stopped for a little extra-curricular activity. Don't know where she got the energy fae,' he concluded, musingly.

He was using up his on the ascent, and went silent till we reached the level ground, stretching forward to Strath na Sealga.

'Sit yer doup on a stane, and we'll hae a rest,' I suggested. We sat, and looked back where we had come, up the birch-filled glen, and then up to the majestic towers of the mountain. I remarked that we were, so far, on our own.

'We'll no be, when we're there,' he asserted. 'The second time I cam here, wis after yon Chris Brasher had done an article in a posh Sunday magazine aboot this place. Said ye could get the train overnight fae London and be there by denner time. There'll be hunners o' the daft English here later in the day.'

I had often noticed that Davie's proletarian internationalism excluded everything that lay between the Tweed and the Channel. But nobody is perfect, and only in his wilder cups, when he would suggest permits for mountain access to be issued in limited numbers at the border, did I put in any token opposition to his Anglophobia. He is one of that band who has never forgiven the English for Flodden, the 9-3 defeat at Wembley, and supremely, Sassenach on Ben Nevis. He talked again of independence as a way of limiting the English invasion.

'Bit Davie,' I countered, 'fa wid look aifter the English if we did that? Naebiddy else wid hae them. It's wir Christian duty.'

Below us was a deep gorge in the river. Davie ventured the opinion that it could be the gorge into which fell one of a party on a celebrated rescue; theme of a recent TV film. It was another peg to hang an attack on the pock-puddens.

'Some upper class type took twa pals on the ridge and lost them doon a gulley when they tried to make their way back. He staggers aff on his ain, fa's doon a gorge, and finally raises the alarm. Patey, fae Ullapool, sets aff in the dark, solo, finds the bodies, wan deid, wan nae, and nearly saves the wan nae deid. Whit happens? The Englishman gets an O.B.E., Patey gets a mention. The English establishment at work!'

I muttered that I had not seen the film, and that we should be moving on, to get to the bothy before the hordes arrived. Just before we moved off he suddenly asked me, 'we, oor generation goin on the hill; wis it the start o' something, or the end o' something?'

'The end o' something,' I said, without hesitation. And we pushed on, hoping to arrive first.

And arrive we did when the place was toom. Davie had promised me beauty, and there it was. Across the strath lay the sandstone towers of Beinn Dearg Mor, shaped like a perfect mountain. Ahead lay the blue of the loch dissolving in a haze that seemed to have nothing behind it. And to the right lay the vast bulk of An Teallach, enticingly hiding its jagged eminences from our eyes. We collected water, drank in our tea and the view. Then strolled to the loch for driftwood. It was on our way back that Davie said, 'look. I telt ye, it's the Redcoats comin.'

I looked up and followed his finger to the mountain's shoulder, where the path debouched to the strath. File upon file of figures were descending to the glen; every now and again another would pop up over the horizon. My democratic pretensions struggled to overcome my horror at the prospect of a bank holiday weekend crush, and I muttered something, I think, about them having as much right to be there as we had.

Davie smiled as he scented my weakening, and said, 'let's get back afore the massed forces o' cultural colonialism get there.'

We counted them in, but stopped at fifty. That night we saw little of them, as we occupied a small back room, and Davie scowled at anyone who approached. The place was big enough to accommodate the others, anyway. In the morning we had an impatient wait, as the others scattered to the four corners of the glen, since we were expecting Young Lochinvar to arrive from his overnight bivouac in his car by the road. He finally arrived to a not-very-friendly greeting from Davie to the effect that his manhood must be wanting, in having taken so long to arrive, and having left the field to the auld enemy.

The new arrival was frog-marched back about a third of the way that he had just come. And we all then started the interminable slog through scree and heather to Sail Liath, the first peak of the ridge, where we caught up with some of our fellow bothiers on the summit. Then on to Corrag Bhuidhe, where a traffic jam had built up at a 30-foot slab that was dripping wet. A couple of parties were getting a rope out for it. Davie was both horrified and pleased.

'I telt ye, the English arnae prepared for this. Aifter yon Lakes and the Peak District, a wee scramble like this frightens the life oot o' them.'

And he scrambled up, leaving us to follow him unceremoniously by jumping our places in the queue. On we went, over the towers of Corrag Bhuidhe and to Lord Berkeley's Seat, where we sat and aristocratically watched the progress of the other mountaineers over the Towers. It was a fine day to dawdle, looking down to the depths of Coire Toll an Lochain.

At Sgurr Fiona, Davie had to be persuaded to go on to Bidean a Ghlas Thuill. Thinking he might be worried about falling behind the national enemy again, I pointed out that these modern mountaineers did not descend till they had done every Munro, Top and Corbett on the ridge, and we duly pressed on. But he drew the line at various outlying tops Young Lochinvar had in mind, and we descended to Loch na Sealga after an invigorating day out. There we broke up driftwood, while Davie pointed out the locations of his amorous escapades by the shore.

At the bothy we had to come out of splendid isolation, as our cubbyhole had no fire; so we lit one in the adjacent big room, leaving our firewood outside. Our fellow occupants came back, exchanged greetings. Everyone messed around, cooking and changing, chatting. By lighting the fire and collecting wood we had assured ourselves of a welcome and squatters' rights. It was a mixed crew; a few cheery Dundonians, some chummy North of England lads, and one sole bothier who sat alone, with glazed look. When he finally spoke, it was to announce the following with rapt intensity: 'every time I go away, I never take an onion. After a while, I get a craving for onions, there must be something in them. I always mean to take away an onion, but I never do, and I get a craving for them.'

It seemed as if he would go on like this forever when I lofted one through the air to land in his lap.

'It's yer lucky day; here's an ingan.'

Everyone was a bit stunned after this and conversation lagged, till a knock came at the door.

'Come in, it's nae locked!' shouted Davie.

In he came, but I think what he said hardly registered.

'Excuse me, is that your wood out there? Could we borrow some to make a fire? You see we haven't brought any with us, and we're rather cold. Also we'd like to cook our meal.'

He could have been out of "Brideshead Revisited": tweed jacket, checked cotton shirt, tweed tie and brogues. The wavy hair, horn-rimmed specs and pipe must have come free with the outfit, to complete the *tout ensemble*. He had obviously forgotten to bring 'his man' with him as well, or he would have sent him with the errand.

There was a silence, deeper than the onion silence. I was all for letting them take some: the lad seemed in a bad way, shivering and twitching. Or maybe he was like that all the time. But I feared Davie's wrath, till he spoke.

'Well, yer supposed tae collect yer ain. It disnae get delivered, ye know. There's tons o' the stuff by the loch. But ye can take enough tae get yersells started.'

Whereupon our supplicant left, and Davie started again.

'That's typical o' the southern English,' he commented, 'the very people that'll be going on aboot dependency culture and stannin on yer ain feet, a' for cutting aff people's social security, and when they come here, takkin' folk's wid.'

I was not quite sure I followed the dialectical logic of this, but I noticed the reference to southern English. For Davie was getting on fine with the northern lads, who had realised he knew a bit about the area, and were interested in doing something over at Carnmore, on Beinn Lair. They were asking his advice — the equivalent, to Davie, of moral virtue. He gave it, mixed with admonition.

'Now jist you lads be careful o' the grades. The Scottish wans are harder. Remember, a Scottish VS is a serious proposition, nae some Lakeland romp.'

The night was passing away merrily, when another knock came at the door. There again stood the Evelyn Waugh creation.

'I'm sorry to trouble you gentlemen again,' he began, 'but we don't seem to be able to get the fire lit. I wonder if you could give us a hand and show us how it's done.'

Silence greeted the question. Davie then got up and exited from the room, without a word. Evelyn followed.

After a while, our Good Samaritan returned, flabbergasted. 'There's dizzens o' Chris Brasher lookalikes ben there,' he gasped. 'They'd tae'n a' oor wid, I'd tae tak maist o' it back aifter I lighted the fire for thcm. They've got wine an smoked salmon. I sent them aff for wid. Nane o' them said a word.'

Davie was obviously seriously distressed by what he had seen. There is a kinder, gentler side to the man, unsuspected by many.

The next morning we met the southrons as we headed off towards Carnmore for the day. I felt some communication was necessary, and asked them where they were going.

'Ben Clayheim,' said one.

'Eh?'

He pointed on the map to Beinn a' Chlaideimh, admittedly a difficult one. But Davie was quick to seize on this, as we were fording the river.

'That's another thing, their cultural imperialism. They mak nae effort tae learn the proper names o' things, or the culture. It's a colonial attitude, pittin the natives in their place.'

As we walked on towards a mountain that Davie insisted on calling Avijin, I gently reminded him that his pronunciation of a certain place near Oban, which he called Tin Drum, was not beyond reproach.

'Aye, but wi' me it's ignorance, wi' them it's arrogance.'

We savoured the walk to Carnmore amidst splendid country, with views of loch and peak all round. Then I left Davie and Lochinvar to test themselves on the crags, while I had a day climbing A'Mhaidghean and Ruadh Stac Mor, sitting a long while atop the latter, and looking down to the Fuar Loch Mor below. We teamed up again in Gleann na Muic Beag, compared notes. Lochinvar was pleased.

'A great couple of climbs,' he said. 'Ecstasy especially.'

'A helluva lang wye, twelve miles round trip, for couple o' hunner feet o' climbing,' was Davie's verdict, but he mellowed. 'There was wan good pitch on it.'

We were late in leaving next day, and eventually had the bothy to ourselves for a leisurely breakfast. Davie watched the retreating Brasherites, deep in thought.

'Aye,' he came away with finally. 'We built their Empire for them, and even now we're still lightin' their fires!'

COLDSVILLE

It would be the coldest night of the century. The next would be colder still.

There had been a long spell of hard frosts, becoming harder. But no new snow had fallen, so the roads were clear as we drove north to the Coe. And lower down the snow covering was quite thin. The ice on lochans and frost on moss and grass contributed more to the sparkling diamante than any snowfall. Low down by the road herded the deer; starved and frozen, hoping for charity, lost of all dignity, like beggars in a city street, like Thatcher's legions.

'Real brass monkey weather,' commented Davie. 'I'll get tae use thae Damarts at last.'

And when we got out of the car, the cold was breathtaking. It was painful to inhale, and we wrapped scarves round mouths to filter the air and ease the cold-induced chest pain, scrabbling back into the vehicle to dress. Though the hut was visible only a couple of hundred yards away, we happed up fully before setting off, scrunching down the frozen slope to the river. We crossed this without noticing it; it had been frozen to a rocklike consistency, and covered with drift, contoured to the moor. We knew that we had crossed when the hut loomed up ahead. There was a light in the window of the 'Ville.

In the van, I stumbled first across the porch and into the hut, after banging my head against the door. While I rubbed my head, the Cerberus of the hut materialised from the shadows, with a welcoming, 'who invited ye in here? This is a Club Hut!'

I looked at the man, coiled like a spring in the shadows. Clearly a street-fighting type, who would do battle at the drop of a wrong word. I continued rubbing my head with one hand, and jerked the other backwards over my shoulder.

'He did.'

Cerberus looked suspiciously over the shoulder, features contorted and mistrustful, then they relaxed.

'Ah, it's you Davie, that's a' right. But ye've tae be careful now. These West Highland Way types are coming in here and shiting everywhere. Come in, we've a fire going.'

It was so cold, and the hut so ill-insulated, that the small fire was of little use except as a source of light. The frost hung thick on the insides of the tarpaulin walls. I meanwhile deposited some coal beside the fire.

'I hope it's no scab coal?' quipped Cerberus, trying to break the ice formed by his initial sally. 'We've been collectin' at the work for the miners.'

'No, it wis bocht afore the strike,' came reassurance. 'And we've been collecting as weel,' I added.

When it was added to the sticks in the grate, a little more heat was given out.

Davie greeted a couple of characters he knew, and they started to make a drum-up.

'There's watter a wee bit doonstream where we've smashed the ice,' we were told by Cerberus. Davie had forewarned me about him, the present guardian of the 'Ville. But he was making such an effort to be friendly that I thought of renaming him Sam the Lamb.

But neither the fire, nor the cooking, nor the breath of men could take the cold from the air, and all soon bedded. Damarts, day gear and two sleeping bags per man kept the lance of the cold at bay. An eerie light from the moon filtered through the windows, frosted on both sides. The fire slowly died.

In the morning there was ice everywhere: the melt and condensation had frozen. Ice on the walls, on the furniture; it crinkled as bodies moved in their iced sleeping bags. Water in bottles had frozen solid. I reached out and felt my boots; they had been recast in iron, unwearable. I took them in beside me in my sleeping bag to thaw.

'Christ, I thocht ye'd only tae dae this in the Himalayas, nae Glencoe.'

As the slow and painful rituals of dressing and eating were undergone, it was agreed: it must have been cold in the night. But of course, everyone knew of a night colder. When the whisky had frozen, when words came out frozen and were melted in the pan, when moustaches and beards snapped off in the cold, and so on.

'It's when the hair in yer nostrils crackles, ye know it's cauld,' was one viewpoint.

As we drove along the road past Cameron's Barn, Davie

pointed to Lagangarbh, the S.M.C. home from home. 'There used tae be an open-cast coal mine there, where the lads managed to get fuel for the fire. Mind you, that didnae go doon too well wi' the S.M.C. I'm surprised the Coal Board hisnae been up working it during the strike.'

'They've got mountains o' the stuff, bigger nor the anes we'll be climbin. Mind you, this weather should help get them burned up,' was my reply.

The day was brilliant, sharp and clear. And cold. But thankfully windless, and without wind chill. Below the house that Hamish rebuilt, we left the car.

'Ye used tae be able tae kip in that byre,' muttered Davie gesturing at an outbuilding. 'But it was stopped. Everything is regulated noo, there's nae room for hoboing any mair.'

He examined the cottage. 'He's dane well for himself, wi' his books and T.V. programmes. Some saw where the chances were, and took them. And some didnae, and are still kipping where we kipped.'

We started up the steep slope to Am Bodach, crampons donned. Though the covering was thin, the ground glittered like tinsel and was hard. But there was snow higher up that we could see. And what more we could see! The wilderness of the Rannoch Moor to the east, like a miniature Arctic ice-cap. To the north the Ben, with the prow of North East Buttress. The Paps of Jura, gorgeous white breasts, like a woman of fantasy, to the south. And nearer, Bidean, where we noticed that there were massive cornices licking the lips of the corries. On reaching the Bodach cairn, there was a debate as to whether the whitened Cuillin we saw was of Rum or Skye. It was of Skye.

Ahead, peak upon peak led to Sgorr Nam Fiannaidh; peak upon peak overlaid with vast cornices, hanging curved over space, like Pacific breakers poised in silent beauty. The snow underfoot was barely scratched by our crampons; there would be a lot of axe work today. And we uncoiled the rope, though we had both done the ridge before without one.

'Wi' it bein sae hard, it'll no avalanche,' said Davie as he prepared to descend the face of Am Bodach to the col, anchored by me. I, however, looking ahead, was not so sure. I had recently read someone who argued on the basis of how a Mars bar broke, that it was more likely to do so when hard, than soft, and that cornices were the same. I ventured this opinion to Davie.

'Look,' he expostulated, 'ye're wi' a man that's taen ye places

35

ye could never get, and taen ye back safely. A man that's got qualifications, certificates. That's been in the Rockies, the Himalayas, and ye're prepared tae doubt me on the basis o' a bloody Mars bar!'

This procured compliance, silence, and a concentration on the belay.

Davie descended, facing the rock, to the col, and anchored himself. He shouted up, 'yer Alpenstock'll no be much use comin doon, but I've made wee steps.'

The disadvantage of a long axe was obvious as I moved down; but Davie's breaking of the surface ice gave purchase to crampons, and a little to mitts, as I came on behind, eyes ignoring the airy drop on either side of the Bodach pinnacle. At the bottom I was quite elated.

'I've done that wi' a lassie, the other wye, a long time ago. It's a lot easier going up.'

Davie looked for a while, then wryly remarked, 'Aye, it's easier getting up wi' a lassie, especially when yer younger.'

Before the ambiguity of this could be resolved we were moving on towards Meall Dearg, linked together with the rope. At first I was so taken with the views, identifying landmarks with wonder, that I did not notice. Of course, I noticed the build-up of snow, and the hardness of it underfoot. But then I also realised that the summit was wider than on my last visit.

The narrow ridge had corniced over, and we were walking on the cornice.

Confirmation definite came when Davie began the scramble over the Pinnacles, or what should have been the Pinnacles, since their summits had grown claws of ice at the fingers, and the gaps between the claws had become webbed with snow: an awful hand, which seemed to have my friend in its grasp. I hoped the lad with the Mars bar had been wrong, as I looked at the emptiness below Davie's feet. I checked my belay, one of those psychological winter ones, and delved again into my reading. Were you not supposed to throw yourself over the other side of a ridge if your companion fell, to establish an equilibrium of forces? I peered down the gully on my left; the cornice at the top looked like it would saw through stone, never mind rope.

But Davie was up and over, and I followed, quicker, in his scoured footsteps. Then we walked with the rope to Stob Coire Leith. The ridge was supposed to be wide here, so all thought of Mars bars was forgotten. Forgotten with the receding of fear, and with the receding of the day. With the departure of day, the light lost its sharpness, became suffused. The hills dissolved into a hazy continuum with the sky. And the sun changed colour from orange to blood as it, briefly, hung above Ben More in Mull before going to bed and switching off the light.

After the Hill of the Fenian Warriors was passed, we had to pick our way slowly down the eroded and iced path at the edge of Clachaig Gully, to avoid slithering into its stygian recesses.

'See that climb,' said Davie. 'If there's somebody ye REALLY dinna like, tell them that's a great climb.'

Darkness had enfolded us on the descent, but stars and a cheesy moon gave enough light, though tiredness was beginning to dull the appetite for beauty and waken that for food. 'No one,' said Goethe, 'can look at the loveliest sunset, after quarter of an hour.'

'It's this bit I hate, walkin' fower miles back up the glen,' came from the ever-cheery Davie when we were back at the roadside. 'We can try hitchin, but naebody'll gie's a lift.'

'Haud on,' I said, halting him. I ignored Davie's query, accompanied by colourful language, as to where I was going, and walked over to a lay-by where three cars were parked. One had a family in it. No use. One was a salesman type. No use. One was a hired car, I noted, with a young couple inside. That's the one, I thought. I chapped at the window, which was rolled down, with a little trepidation.

'Excuse me, sorry to trouble you, but we've just been along the Aonach Eagach ridge, and I've twisted my ankle. I wonder if you'd be so kind as to give my companion and myself a lift back to our car, four miles up the glen.'

The lad looked unsure. His companion was momentarily speechless. Then she said, in amazement, 'you've been up THERE?' pointing to the ridge. She was impressed. I tried to look modest. The lad then mumbled agreement. So I went to fetch Davie, prickling with embarrassment on his rucksack like a hedgehog.

Back at our car, we thanked our saviours, and alighted. Davie had been unusually quiet for the four miles. But as he started his own vehicle, he turned and said, 'aye, ye've got yer uses, after a'.'

We decided to go straight to the pub and eat there. It seemed to be getting colder by the minute. The sky was brilliantly clear as we headed for the hospitality of the hostelry. Behind the bar was the man who had done Zero Gully and Point Five on the Ben before his dinner, and who would one day do the North-east Ridge of Everest.

'Hullo, Davie, how's things?' he cried. 'Staying over bye?' — and he pulled a couple of pints and took our orders. I was stunned. Here I was, almost bathing in the reflected glory of the famous. I tried to look as if I knew the barman too. To look casual, as if the question of the breaking strain of Mars bars never crossed my mind.

'It was minus 22 last night,' announced the barman, when the food was brought, 'and it'll be colder tonight.'

It was a normal night in the bar. Some played darts, some swapped tales, some sat round a lad with a guitar who sang a few songs. The pints were quaffed and the evening wore on, till round midnight the barman of fame decided that all must wend their ways home.

Leaving was like walking into a deep freeze; once before — only once — I experienced that feeling, when walking into a frozen fish store in a filleting factory. We ran to the car, with sharp daggers of pain twisting in our chests; the hairs in my nostrils crinkled. I could feel, imagined I could hear them! We stood by the car, while Davie searched every pocket for his keys. On finding them, he could not touch the metal of the car lock, and pulled his sleeve down over his hand. Dropped the keys. Picked them up again. Fumbled with the lock.

'I'm going to die,' I thought, hopelessly, as the pain in my chest became so unbearable that I tried not to breathe. But we got in, and by some miracle the machine started first time, speeding us back to the hut car park. It had been a mistake to change out of hill gear when we had come off the hill, and we donned it once again for the short trip to the hut. We made no attempt to light a fire, but crawled quickly into the life-preserving double sleeping bags.

Returned home the next day, we discovered that it had fallen to minus 29, the coldest night of the century; the coldest night for a century and more.

'Ye missed yer chance,' said Davie.

'Fit for?'

'Tae try an experiment for yer theory aboot Mars bars, under perfect conditions.'

COCKALEEKIE

'Ye've tae decide. Are ye a man o' the West, or are ye still hankering after yer lost youth in the East?'

I considered the words, as I stared at the night sky above the Devil's Elbow. A fine night, a crisp winter's night. Davie was like that: a simple trip ended in becoming a philosophical controversy. You could not just suggest going to the 'Gorms for a change; oh, no, lurking behind this must be some profound objective you were concealing, possibly even from yourself. The argument that in Sputan Dearg there were some nice wee winter climbs — nothing too hard — that was merely an alibi for some ulterior motive.

But I needed most of my attention for the drive on the rimed road. The old chevvy (vette, not rolet) with a hole in one wing that looked like a cannonball had done it, and the spongy brakes, was not exactly clinging to the road on the ascent to the pass. I thus could not spare enough effort for a reply, and had to give him free rein to continue his theme. Which he did, with some story about north-east misanthropy that had befallen him the last time he had been to Bob Scott's bothy, wounding the delicate philanthropic soul that lurked in his own west coast breast. Something to do with somebody using his candle. He was in the middle of this when we passed Callater, and I decided on deflection tactics.

'We used tae ging tae a fine wee bothy up that glen . . .'

More ammunition against the east coast.

'Fine wee bothy! I've been there. We went on a Creag Dhu smoker weekend. David Todd's idea, but he never came, he knew better. Lost a couple o' guys in the snaw, and picked them up alive on the wye oot in the morning. It was a hovel, nae roof and stane fleer, full o' horse shite. The lads a' left first thing in the morning . . .'

I interrupted, smirking: 'Aye, yer Creag Dhu pals arnae tough enough for the Cairngorm bothies, it seems.'

We were in the Fife Arms quaffing pints before he had time to recover from shooting himself in the foot. Sitting by the fire, lousing his belt and looking radiantly content, he continued, 'mind you, I'm no feelin sae weel. This funny hollowness . . .'

'It's the drink, Davie.'

'Naw, naw, it's no the drink. I think it's yon disease that's going aboot, it's ca'ed cockaleekie, or something like that. Davie Provan, the Celtic player, has got it. Ye're tired a' the time, and ony exertion wears ye oot; taks years tae recover.'

Now he mentioned it, I had been feeling the same, and said so.

'Ach, you! You're jist a hypochondriac, naething the maitter wi' you!'

We left.

And as we set off up Glen Derry, it seemed as if the cold had killed the cockaleekie bug. We felt invigorated, drinking in the air that smelt of iron and tasted of chablis. We fairly trotted up the glen, despite mega-packs of ropes, winter climbing gear, provisions and sacks of coal and kindling. Through the dark Derry woods we went, I pointing out youthful mementoes in places by the road, the back route to Mar Lodge.

'That's why ye're a' sae bad-tempered. Yer bothies are a' hunners o' miles fae the road, and youse never could spend enough time in the boozers. Are we nearly there? I can feel the cockaleekie coming on.'

We were, but as they had moved the bridge (in fact, they had moved the whole river) since I was last there, it took us a little while longer to get to the hallowed portals of the most famous shed in the world.

'I've been here afore, ye know. This is no the first time,' said Davie, not for the first time.

But never when the old man Scott had been there. Almost 15 years ago at that time since the warm-hearted but irascible old gamekeeper, who ruled his bothy like a feudal superior, had moved out of the house nearby. Now there was no one in the shuttered house, or, as we discovered, in the bothy itself. Already drunk with the air and the walk, I made a heady cocktail for myself of the paraphernalia, old and new, of the doss. I was not sure I approved of the bunks. But there was Desperate Dan's old cane chair, and the tilly lamp was still hanging on the rafters. The Bluecol advert, with the wee robin in the snowdrift, was still on the mantelpiece . . . I began to feel quite sappy and sentimental all of a sudden. When I tried to convey this to Davie, he looked worried.

'Maybe ye are sickenin for something aifter a',' he conceded.

It was late. And cold, how cold. So we went straight to bed. But it was a long time before I stopped looking at the sky through the frame of the window, cloudless. Here I was, coming back to do some 'easy' winter climbs on Sputan Dearg where I had done my first easy rock climbs 20 years before.

Maybe there was something in what Davie had been saying at the Deil's Elbae . . .

I listened to the murmur of the river. I listened to the trees fanning across the roof of the bothy. And slept.

In the morning the mist had come down, and we both felt very lethargic as we breakfasted. I crunched across the snow to the ice-fragmented water, and looked up towards the Lairig Ghru; a few flakes of snow drove me indoors. Davie had the breakfast on. We seemed to take forever to eat it, and then get packed up for the hill. I felt heavy, but hollow as well. We tramped off up the hard path, dusted with a smirr of snow. Slowly.

'I'm wabbit,' I ventured.

'Me tae,' mused Davie.

But we moved on. Slowly. Till we saw the cottonwool mist filling Sputan Dearg Corrie, and took the path into the deepening snow which lay like a bandage on the mountain.

Davie stopped.

'Gie's yer shulder,' he panted.

And we supported each other for a while, like two drunks, before moving on. And on. Slowly.

Eventually we decided that we must be near the foot of the crag, and we veered westwards into the cottonwool. Sure enough, the base of some rocks emerged from the wool, above the bandage, like a black scar on a wound. Ugly rocks lay there, waiting for us to do something.

'It's the fit of a climb,' said Davie, 'but, whit wan?'

I was content to sit down, breathing hollowly, and let him work it out from the guidebook. I hoped it would take him a long time. While he pondered I ate frosted apricots and snow.

'I think,' announced Davie, 'that this is Slab Chimney.'

'I think,' I said, after waiting a while to answer, 'that ye've got absolutely nae evidence for saying that.'

I asked Davie what the Gude Book said.

'All pitches may disappear after heavy snow,' he quoted.

'That's a lot o' help,' I replied.

I dozed. Dreamed. And in the dream we were climbing through mist on cottonwool snow, scooping our way up silently to the plateau above . . . But when I suddenly jerked into waking we were not above the cornice, but still sitting at the bottom, Davie flicking the pages of the guidebook for inspiration. I heard him saying, 'it could be Slab Chimney, but it might be Ardath Chimney.'

I had as much interest in that question as I had about the topography of the dark side of the moon, and conveyed this to him, though in less elaborate language.

Let's get doon the hill,' I suggested. 'If we bide here I'll fa asleep, and this is the kind o' situation fan ye fa asleep, ye wakkin up deid.'

He agreed wordlessly, packing his gear.

'I wonder whit yon route was?' he mused as we moved off.

I could not have given tuppence to know. I was hollow, dizzy and tired. We wobbled off downhill, led by the compass, and emerged below the mist at Sron Riach. Then combined tactics were used: we supported each other as we snailed back to the bothy, leaving an erratic trail in the snow.

'Maybe it's the onset o' the menopause,' Davie ventured, 'maybe nature is tryin' tae tell us somethin? Maybe my winter climbing days are done.'

I began to dream of the fireplace, and sleep; not food, just sleep.

This time, Scott's was full. We came in, rimed and roped, to meet the gazes of a party of young lads. English walkers doing the Lairig Ghru, who had come on from Corrour, which was full up. A little adrenalin began to flow, and so too did a lot of whisky. They ceded us seniority and the chairs by the fire for the evening, due to our prior occupancy.

'Nice tae see the young lads sae respectful,' beamed Davie.

'Aye, they'll be gieing ye their seats on the buses next,' I chipped in.

And they listened, as younger men will, to older ones who have entered dramatically from the field of manly endeavour, to tales of fights on the slippery verticals.

'You must have been here before, then?' queried a fresh-faced loon.

I paused for maximum impact, revelling in attention. Then said: 'ye see yon tin sign there, with the spurdie on't? Abune the lum, there? Well, that wis there fan ye were a glint in yer Daddie's e'e, the first time I seen it.'

And then I felt more amazed than he was. I was his age when I first sat here, and he was not born. Now my own son was born, and I was not any more a young man. I changed the subject.

Next day the cockaleekie had abated a bit, and we strolled down to the car at the Linn. The cockaleekie came and went, then went. But so did any further attempts at the winter climbing.

'But there's still the rock climbing; ye've mony a classic V.Diff tae dae,' was Davie's consoling footnote. 'And I'll gie ye a tight rope.'

'Fine, if we can get ye doon fae fowerteen stanes,'. I ribbed, giving the Flexible Friend above his waist a friendly nudge.

And he did; and we did.

FIRE AND ICE

'A key, ye can get a key?' queried Davie unbelievingly.

'Nae bother,' I replied with more confidence than I really possessed.

This promise persuaded the two Young Doctors to accompany us on a midwinter penetration of the wilderness around Ben Alder. I had met a lad on a hill in summer who had said that the Ben Alder gamie let climbers have a key to the private road to Ben Alder Lodge. This would allow us to get to Culra bothy, and spend the weekend on the surrounding hills, since it would save us a seven-mile walk. As our couple of cars stopped at Dalwhinnie, and I wandered up to the gamie's cottage, I reflected on the fact that I always seemed to expose myself to being hoist with my own petard. It did seem unlikely that any estate would pursue this policy. I mean, to most of them we were classed along with foxes, eagles and other creatures dubbed 'vermin'.

I chapped the door. A woman came, and I started clumsily telling the story about the key. She cut me short.

'It jist hings there,' pointing to the door frame. 'Jist pit it back fin yer feenished.'

And she closed the door against the bitter cold.

I took the key nonchalantly and went back to the car.

'Contacts,' I said, as the company stared in wonder. 'It's contacts ye need in this game.'

We bumped over the railway, and along to the gate, unlocked it and proceeded cautiously along Loch Ericht, for it was a bumpy road, and on this night, an icy one. No one fancied a nosedive into the loch below. It was a fine night when we left the cars near the Lodge and started the walk to Culra. Before Loch Pattack we disturbed hundreds of hungry deer on the flats, searching for some sustenance in the frozen vegetation. The loch gleamed, an oilspill on the moor, as we turned south towards the bothy crunching the forming ice underfoot. To the

44

south of the wedge of the Bealach Dubh was star-filled and the moon streamed in the window all night.

The morning was as fine as the night, for once. A windy day, and with the cloud high. Snow had fallen, and so too had the temperature. We returned to Loch Pattack and found it already freezing over. Thence we headed west towards Beinn a' Chlachair, the stonemason's hill. The walk was not difficult, but it was bracing against the wind, especially once we stood on the plateau. Near the top it was icy enough to get the axes out for balance. At the cairn we stopped a brief while. Davie was looking northwards, then spoke, 'that cannae be Binnein Shuas, is it?'

When told that it was, he was puzzled.

'But it's beside Fort William, this is the ither side o' the country!'

'Ah bit, Davie, a' the different bits jine up. They're jist separate on the maps,' I corrected him.

And that day we could see the different bits. The white Cairngorm plateau to the east, Ben Nevis with its ridges to the south, and to the west, could that be Sgurr na Ciche?

We had seen not a living thing, man or beast, on the way out, nor did we on the way back. Only the grass moved pale yellow against the snow, aside from ourselves, who moved over it, a little slower now. By the loch we began to forage for wood, as we would need a fire that night. Pulling the bog pine out of the freezing peat, we filled our packs with it. Tired now, we did not speak, just looked round every corner for the bothy. I had pulled a muscle, and it had stiffened with the cold. I walked in pain behind the rest, dreaming of the fire, of whisky. Davie dropped back to me, and carried my wood.

We arrived and deposited our foraging on the existing pile. Inside it was clear we had visitors. A group of young men and women sat closely around a very small fire. The Young Doctors were already cooking. It was clear the ice had not been broken, indeed, it was hardening. There was muttering in stage whispers about people hogging the fire, while the new party were going through an elaborate melodrama which seemed to assert that they had done some repairs on the bothy, and thus had a prior right to its usage. I took four Disprin and a couple of drams, and then, in mild euphoria, suggested we wait till we had eaten before doing anything. Maybe they would get the message?

But they did not. We changed and ate, and still they sat there round their feeble fire. Ice was forming from condensation inside the windows of the bothy, and the atmosphere was becoming a permafrost. Then one of the other party got up and went out, coming back with a new supply of wood: our wood! We all stared in amazement at the temerity of it. Then the Young Doctor surged forward, scattering the enemy in all directions.

'Right, if you are using our wood, you'll let us in by the fire. Here, you, move over, you get back. Make space over there. Davie, Ian, Paul, bring over some seats.'

The Blitzkrieg was so overwhelming that we were soon all sat round the fire in amazement. We were as much surprised as the enemy, since the Young Doctor is the mildest-mannered of men normally. He then took charge of the fire, banking it up, feeding the heart, and stacking the damp wood to dry. Soon, though the social ice remained, the fire spread its glow. The heat and the whisky dulled the pain in my leg.

I tell this story to make a moral. Our behaviour was entirely justified, given the boorishness of the company we met. But more social skill on our part might have had better results. I recall a night more recently when our party came back from a 16-mile midwinter's hike in the Cairngorms to Feshie bothy. We had headed for Monadh Mhor, but failed to cross the raging Eidart Burn. We were disappointed to find another party, just arrived, in possession as we entered, cold, hungry, dispirited. They too huddled round a small fire as we cooked, and they too made no move. Some of our party were for going straight to bed, but another tried, explained we had collected wood which we were willing to share, that we were cold, and that there was room for all.

'When you finish your meal, we'll rearrange the seating.'

They made room sheepishly, apologising for their thoughtlessness. We joined them, and shared our drink around. Tales were told, a song or two sung, and the night lasted will the wee sma oors. All were the gainers.

Next day I was in agony, and hirpled back to the car with Paul, while Davie and the Young Doctor set out for Lancet Edge for a snow and ice romp before going back. They hacked their way up the Edge, and were then engulfed in a spindrift blizzard on the plateau, forcing descent to the Bealach Dubh.

I was delighted with myself, despite the muscle. The key had transpired, and I had taken the lads to a new area which had impressed them with its scale. Davie, however, was not one for dispensing gratuitous praise. I have already mentioned his weird ideas of geography. In the car going back, he commented, 'Aye, that's the last twice we've been up the east coast. Maybe we'll get goin away the west coast some time . . .'

THE RIDGE AND THE MIDGE

That leaden sky, like something hammered out in a sheet metal workshop. That tatty distillery, flaked white against the sky. And no lift, nothing to get us to Glen Brittle.

The bus driver had told us to wait; his brother would take us over the hill from Carbost. So we waited. A few drops of rain fell. The village idiot appeared — not our driver, surely? But he passed on. Then it stopped. A van, not the rain. Without number plates, without seat belts, and, as we later discovered, without brakes. But with a driver. A drunk one. As we moved forwards with a mixture of anxiety and expectation, he motioned us to wait. A couple of minutes later he appeared from a shop, half bottle disappearing into a pocket which was trying to resist taking it.

'This'll be the maist dangerous thing in the trip,' mused Davie, and I felt inclined to agree.

The road was as narrow and twisting as the Ridge we were aiming for. But the driver knew it well enough, even in his semi-inebriated state, crawling along at walking pace. And using the handbrake to slow down further, at corners and when other vehicles appeared. Or maybe it only went that fast, I thought as we crawled. A collie dog peeped in whiles from the back to see what was going on. We met little en route, and arrived safely at Glen Brittle. On being asked what he was owed, the driver replied, 'oh, nussing at all. It wass a pleasure haffing you lads.' Adding quickly as we descended, 'but if you would chust like to be giffing a chentleman somesing to trink your health, it would be most welcome.'

It was cheap at the price.

We raced through the campsite and along the path above the shore, towards Gars Bheinn. The rain had relented, but it was sticky, close, and that sky was still pressing down heavily. Sweat soon poured from us . . . mixing with a soft drizzle which began to fall. Midges drowned in their thousands in the liquid mixture. Heavy sky, heavy steps, and countless irritations. We decided to go high to escape the midges, and bivouac on Coire an Laoigh, below Gars Bheinn. Davie stretched a bivvy sheet over a rock, tying boulders to the corners, to make a shelter.

'A mate o' mine in America taught me this. He learned it in Vietnam,' said Davie, proud of his labours.

'Aye, but he'd only the Vietcong tae deal wi'; we've got the midges,' I replied.

'Did Erchie Boomer ivver tell ye the story o' when he was on the John Muir trail in America, and he met this redneck GI fae Vietnam? Saw Erchie eating rice, and said he'd nivver survive on that. Back comes Erchie, "aye, weel, that's whit the Vietcong eat, and they're no daein sae bad against youze!" '

Soon we had caught a cool uplift breeze, and this blew the midges away. We downed a few drams, and started a fitful sleep.

Eyes opened periodically, to heavy skies, cloud. A wind rose and fell. Stars blinked in the dark.

And then morning, 6 a.m. A real morning, with the colours in place. Blue sky joining a green sea, and brown islands bobbing in the waves. Above us, sculpted pinnacles, black. It looked as if the slate had been wiped clean, and everything started again. But as we toiled up a weary slope to gain Sgurr nan Eag, dreams of a second Eden faded with the colours, as the day became overcast, close. What we had in mind would be drouthy work.

Abraham had argued 100 years ago that anyone doing the Cuillin Ridge would 'need to have exceptional physique and staying power, to be a quick, skilful and neat rock climber'. Shadbolt and Maclaren had taken nearly 17 hours on the first traverse, but now Beardie had done it in less than five hours, solo. Patey had called the first Winter Traverse 'the greatest single adventure in British mountaineering'. We did not aspire to that, but Davie and I did feel that the summer traverse was within our powers, and could be done in about ten hours from where we stood on Sgurr nan Eag, to Sgurr nan Gillean.

We knew that water was a problem. The soilless rock of the Cuillin holds none, and there is no spring till Bruach na Frithe. So we had filled plastic bottles with the liquid at camp, keeping it for later in the day. A day which became increasingly sultry and humid. Sweat oozed out of us.

'Gets mair like Vietnam a' the time,' quipped Davie.

We passed Caisteal a' Gharbh Choire, and scrambled up Sgurr Dubh na da Bheinn, pausing to look towards the Sgurr Dubh

Mor ridge, black and jagged to the east. Then, making good time, arrived above the Thearlaich Dubh gap, we found our first difficulty. The rain of the previous day had left the gap sodden, and we slithered rather than rappelled into it. With the rock wet and worn smooth, getting out was a slippery business.

'It must hae been easier when Collie did it — still rough,' said Davie as he struggled for secure grip.

'Aye, and he failed the first time as weel,' was the encouragement he got.

But the leader now had the makings of it. Jamming his dry rucksack against the wall for purchase, he backed upwards. And the second soon followed. The rucksack looked a bit wet, but we assumed this was from the wet walls of the gap.

Despite the drooking we had got in the gap we were still hot and sticky, and parched with thirst. Three hours had gone by since water passed our lips. On top of Sgurr Thearlaich we stopped to drink. Here we recalled the good days. That on the Coire Lagan round, when we came up through the mist to see the Cuillin archipelago, floating above the clouds, dipping in and out of cloud and sun as we went. That when we had followed the nail scars of Steeple and Barlow, on Direct Route, below us on East Cioch Buttress.

'Murray's right: yon was much harder than V.Diff. I've done easier severes,' said Davie, rummaging in the haversack for the water. But then his tone and topic changed.

'It's soaking inside here, my clais are wringing weet.'

And the horrible truth hit us both at the same time: the rucksack back-up had burst the water bottles. The precious liquid was dropping, muckily, from the bottom of the sack. Not a drop was left.

'Maybe it'll rain,' said Davie.

'Maybe.'

Chastened, we moved on. At Sgurr Mic Coinnich we halted below King's Chimney.

'Let's go roond by Collie's Ledge, it's quicker,' suggested Davie. 'Withoot watter we'll need tae hurry.'

We circuited the peak by the natural corridor traversing below the summit.

'If this was Italy, there'd be laidders, ropes and auld wifies staggering aboot,' said Davie.

It didn't sound a bad idea to me.

Over An Stac, and to the foot of the Pinnacle of Sgurr Dearg came the thirsty party, tongues cleaving to the roofs of our mouths as in the Bible. Here Davie summoned up all his skills of leadership.

'I know ye'll be wanting tae dae this, for yer Munroes,' he said, trying to sound sympathetic to this Salvationist obsession from his Ultramontane orthodoxy, 'but we'll jist hae tae skip by: Without watter we cannae eat, and without eating we'll get weak. Speed is the only wye we can dae this.'

I wearily demurred, seemingly with reluctance, but secretly with delight. The Pinnacle did look awfully steep and exposed. We scrambled up the flank of the long side of the Pinnacle to rest briefly at its base. Here we met the first fellow mountaineers of the day, up on a trip from Glen Brittle.

Then I had an idea to lessen our plight. Davie was horrified by it, and he moved away, pretending not to be with me. The idea was this. With a wheedling hard luck story, I would scrounge water from the day trippers to allow us to continue the Traverse. I obtained a little fluid, reluctantly parted with, and returned to share it with Davie, whose objections to its method of procurement did not extend to refusal to drink it. Then I went on my rounds again.

'Excuse me, we're trying the Ridge, and we've lost our water. I'd be obliged if you could spare us some?'

Suddenly from behind me I heard, 'I've better nor that for ye.'

Turning, I all but keeled over. There was Fishgut Mac, a man I had not clapped eyes on for ten years, smiling and holding out a can of beer for me and another one for Davie. As we quickly exchanged greetings, news and promises to renew contact, we gulped the frothy beer, which raised our spirits and hopes.

'This is Fishgut Mac, Davie,' I introduced them. 'Mind that man I telt ye was rebuilt fae scratch by the National Health?'

But the beer was a bad idea. As we rushed on, scrambling over Banachdich, Sgurr a' Ghreadaidh and Sgurr a' Mhadaidh, the alcohol produced headaches and dizziness. On the South West peak we tried to eat; the food crumbled in our mouths and fell out. We rested awhile.

'It's three quarters done,' insisted Davie. 'Eight peaks bagged oot o' eleven. Two-three hours and we'll be there.'

'Two-three hours and I'll be deid. I'm three quarters done as weel. Look at that river doon there.'

A thousand feet below, white water crested in falls, luring us down. The decision was made without speech. Through rock

and scree and boulders we stumbled down, eyes never off the water. Finally we all but fell into it, gallons of it flowing over us and into us.

Later, on the bank, there was not much to say.

'Bad luck that.'

'Aye.'

The worst was over, the torments of thirst slaked. As we descended, the sun came out weakly. We arrived at the Youth Hostel; nothing now but to hitch a lift back to Sligachan, where waited the tent, pitched to greet the victors on return. A party of French schoolgirls passed us on the path. They were bare-legged and scented, wearing summer frocks. We mountaineers felt dirty and unwashed; we were. Nothing passed, no cars appeared.

Then, like a light being switched off, the sun dipped behind a hill. That instant billions of midges appeared. We donned more clothes, moved about to get relief. Billions more appeared. One of us took a turn sheltering in the Hostel lobby while the other hitched.

'I'd rather be back on yon ridge, wi' the thirst, than this,' wailed Davie, tormented. He was not the only one.

The French lassies appeared in a riot of frocks and screams, waving wildly as they fled back to the Hostel, their bare flesh lush pastures for the midges. Even in his agony, Davie managed, as he watched the girls, 'at times ye can envy the midges.'

In desperation, I forcefully flagged down the first car that passed. It was the second time to beg that day. The window opened, and a million midges entered to settle on the startled American couple. Nevertheless, they took pity and gave us mountaineers a lift back to Sligachan. Back at the tent, too tired and miserable to eat, we hit the hay.

In the morning, decamp and a wait for the bus at the Hotel. The bus was late, the midges came out again. The pub was closed, there was no shelter. No, not again!

'Tae hell wi' this,' I uttered to Davie. 'Come wi' me.'

And I led into the front door of the Hotel. Davie reluctantly followed.

'Whit's this? I've been coming here twenty years, and never set fit anywhere but the Public Bar!'

'We might have been defeated on the Ridge, but we'll imitate the great pioneers in another wye.'

'Whit?'

For answer, I pressed a button, and a waitress in pinafore appeared.

'Morning coffee and scones for two please, in the Lounge!'

There we were, if not in the footsteps, in the bum prints of Collie, Abraham, the Pilkingtons and others, stuffing scones and watching the Cuillin from the window, admiring the paintings, and having gentlemanly chat. By the time the bus came, it did not seem so bad after all.

'Next time we try the Ridge, we'll bide in the Hotel.'

'And read the old visitor's books by the fire. They'd be some reading!'

We paused a while.

'Will there be a next time?'

'Oh, aye. The Cuillin will aye be there. They winnae go awa. And neither will the midgies.'

SPECIAL OFFER

'It'll be expensive, and besides, I don't like being away from my car.'

I had suggested to Davie a trip away to the hills by train. Like many others, Davie was a firm believer in public transport — in theory. But like many others he always had a specific reason why he should have a licence to blast holes in the ozone layer and add to the greenhouse effect. In vain I enticed him with tales of the wonderful trips I had had by train over the years. So I decided on a new tack which I knew would appeal to him.

'There's a special offer. Five pounds return anywhere in Scotland. And I've got the wife tae agree tae drive us tae the station.'

This left him without a leg, or a wheel, to stand on, and he agreed, especially after I had suggested a trip over the moor to Corrour, and then on to Ben Alder cottage.

'I've no been there for nearly twenty years,' he mused. 'I was chatting tae wee Onie,' he continued, 'and he was telling me that the Auld Crowd hired a boat and outboard and went in there at New Year, up Loch Ericht in the teeth o' a storm. Ye mind when Murray went there, in *Undiscovered Scotland*, and met a group o' Glesca poachers? I think yon wis the Auld Team. . . .'

In the train, he was like a wee boy, hardly able to keep still. But once it crawled its way out of Glasgow, he settled down to survey the scenery, the views of the Cobbler and Ben Lomond near Tarbert finer than available from the roadside: straight across to the corrie of the former, and then back, to the northern arete-like side of the latter. As he bounded from side to side of the vehicle, I suggested, 'Awa an ask the guard if he'll let ye blaw the whistle, Davie.'

We chatted in the train to a group of fishermen getting systematically drunk in the buffet: the fish appeared to have little to fear. They got off with us at Corrour, and, somewhat unsteadily, started off after the vanishing lights of the train. I hoped there were no more trains due that night. They were making for a railway hut further along the track at Loch Treig; we halted for the night at one barely a mile north of Corrour Station. These huts were built as shelters for the men maintaining the line, and several still provide good watertight accommodation in remote spots.

We stretched out along the benches, got the stoves out, got some food on. A dram or two and a chat as the candle was lit; we were asleep before it guttered. Unmoving in slumber. Until the earthquake unleashed by the morning train to Glasgow at 6 a.m. awoke us with a start.

We passed by the station again, and the Youth Hostel, where there were signs of bustle, and decided to part for a while. Davie was a little out of condition, and at that stage where he seriously doubted whether lumbering up big wet lumps was a suitable substitute for a diminishing climbing career. So he had a lovely day. Wandering along the sand-fringed shore of Loch Ossian, past the heronry and through the mixed birch and pine woods. Ascending towards the Bealach Dubh on the horizon, then cutting across to gain the fine stalkers' path that descended to Ben Alder cottage. Here he 'hewed wood and drew water' till my arrival, and professed himself delighted with his day. I, meanwhile, was taking a route to the bothy over the tops.

Gradual ascent by the path known as the Road to the Isles took me onto the shoulder of Carn Dearg, and a long pull led me to the summit cairn. It was hazy and oppressive, and little was to be seen bar the deer which I disturbed with great frequency. I remembered that the shooting season had started, hoping that in the mist I did not look like a stag.

The Mam Ban between the peaks was rutted with peat hags, through which I navigated, to reascend the easy slope to the summit of Sgor Gaibhre. On a fine day there would have been a view, I thought bitterly, descending once again to the bealach, and facing the final pull up to Sgurr Choinnich. It was only a top, not a peak; I wished I could miss it out. Maybe Davie had the right idea, after all.

Bang! Bang! Bang! In a panic, I dropped like a stone, trying impossibly to locate the source of the shots in the mist. I lay there, cold and afraid, and then I heard the sound of muffled voices coming from the col below. A couple of hairy jackets, dripping with moisture, emerged from the mist. It was Milord and his Lady, smiling sweetly as one does for the lower classes.

But they waited for the equally soaking ghillie to arrive and communicate. He adopted a polite but firm tone.

'We didn't expect anyone on the hill today. It's the shooting season, and dangerous in this mist. Lord and Lady —— would be pleased if you didn't go in our direction.'

'Where are you headed?' I asked hopefully. The aristocrats still smiled, and remained silent. How nice, I thought, to have another to do all one's unpleasantness.

'We are following the beasts to Sgurr Choinnich,' the ghillie replied.

'I was going there,' I replied, 'but I'll just descend to Ben Alder cottage, instead.'

I chuckled inwardly on the descent by Loch a' Bhealaich, and on the tramp across mud flats to the bothy. Here I found my pal already ensconced, and the welcoming fire on. I sat with a dram, and told Davie of my encounter on the tops. And this brought to mind a story about an uncle of my wife's. He was a seasonal worker on that very estate, down from Skye with a gang of labourers in the inter-war years. There was no work on the island, and they were planting the Loch Ossian forest. The then lady of the manor expected a deference from the workers they were unprepared to give; Caley finally told her to 'go to hell'. He was dragged by the estate manager before her ladyship and told to apologise, or be sacked.

'Apologise for saying "Go to hell",' was the order.

'Alright, you don't have to go *now*,' came the reply.

The next day the weather was worse, and a gale-force wind had got up. We trudged dutifully up to the col between Ben Alder and Ben Bhoil, heads down. Then we buffeted, backs to the wind, till we reached the summit ridge of the latter hill. By this time it was difficult to stand, and Davie decided to withdraw to replenish the wood supplies.

With five hundred feet to go I was on all fours, looking for handholds as one does on a rock climb; a hundred to go and I was on my stomach, crawling towards the summit cairn. I pulled myself into its lee, and rested. There was a boiling storm on Loch Ericht below. On the descent I was hurled by the wind, and took flying leaps over rocks and boulders.

In the bothy, the fire again. And Davie telling a young lad sitting listening with rapt attention, and obvious relief, that there was not a ghost. McCook, the last occupant of the cottage, had not committed suicide. A couple with a tent arrived, and sent their young children into the bothy to dry by the fire, with apologies to us. We gave the young man a dram, and told the children tales of McCook, Cluny the Jacobite who had a cave on Ben Alder, and of that other mythical figure, Wee Onie. They listened popeyed, and were dragged back by their parents, dry but protesting, to the tent.

In the morning, it was clear that the young man had decided, unbidden, to come with us. He packed, and waited for us to do so. Then he followed us down Loch Ericht at a respectful distance. We lunched at a fishermen's hut on the Rannoch Moor, and he shared our company unbidden. I wondered if he was going to try and come home with us, like a lamb that once followed me off the Cobbler.

Across the moor we could see the line and the Rannoch Station, which we wearily attained after a river crossing. On its platform we snapped the approach of the Iron Horse, and meditated on the men who built it. A memorial to its chief engineer stands at the station. Setting off from Loch Treig head in frock coats and umbrellas, the original survey party hit bad weather and were lost for two days; they survived by a miracle, or Victorian fortitude.

On the way back we witnessed a huge traffic jam at Crianlarich from the buffet of the train.

'Fools, fools,' mused my companion, looking pityingly at the drivers, as he downed another dram. We managed to exhaust the train's whisky supplies, and still had change over what the full fare would have cost us, which gave Davie great satisfaction.

We lost our wee boy somewhere on the journey home. One of them.

THE ASCENT OF NYMPHET CRACK

We were trudging up the Buttermilk Burn on what promised to be a heavenly day: blue skies, fluffy clouds, a light breeze. Davie had been fulminating against those, the majority, who ascended the Cobbler on the alternative route, by the base of the old overhead railway. This, along with Hearts not having won a trophy for thirty years, and the improvement to the Loch Lomond Road ('the Nine Bends, that ye got roon by accelerating at every wan'), were all lumped together in a general *Kulturkritik* of modern civilisation as we ascended. I saved my breath for the ascent, knowing that Davie would have no trouble filling the silence I left for him.

The wood was fresh with bluebells and primroses by the burn; light filtered through the bright green leaves of May. It was very romantic. And Davie began a story. I cannot remember if it was the one about the Himalayas or the Rockies, or just Scotland; but it did not matter, since it was always the same story. Innocently intent on ascending the heights, Davie would be assailed by some beautiful young woman who pressed her attentions on him. Despite his resistance, she succeeded, and adopted a great interest in climbing. But just when he thought he had found the woman of his dreams she started finding excuses for not going away of weekends. And trudging round jewellery shops, looking at diamond rings, the terrible truth would dawn on him about her intentions. The boots would be hung up and schemes of homemaking take the place of dreams of expeditions.

'Wummen,' he said disgustedly. 'Ye tak them tae bothies and they start measuring the windaes up for curtains! There's nane o' them really interested in the hills.'

By this time we had reached the Narnain Boulder and in the growing heat we stopped for a rest. The *Kulturkritik* continued.

'Look at that, jist dubs inside, and the wall tummeled doon. Ye couldnae doss in that noo. Naebody sleeps up here noo, it's a day-tripper's hill. Auld Jock Nimlin would be turning in his grave if he could see this.'

'But he's nae deid yet Davie,' I corrected. (He was not, at the time.)

'I was being poetic. He spent mair nichts howffing up here than ye've had hot denners. Naebody knew this mountain like him. It's one o' his routes we're daeing the day.'

'Fit ane?'

'Recess Route. Just a V.Diff., but he says it's the best route on the mountain, the best in the area. The crux is severe though, so ye'll need a tight rope. There'll be naebody on it; it's beneath the dignity o' these modern tigers. They are a' muscles and nae imagination.'

Davie himself knew the Cobbler hardly less than did Nimlin. Possibly even better, since he had done many of the routes added since Nimlin's day — bar the elusive Club Crack which he stared at wistfully on every visit. I myself found Cobbler climbing horrendously hard, depending as it does on balance on fine holds; but he assured me that Recess was more muscular, and more suited to a man who liked jumping for jugs, as I did.

Further up, we investigated the High Doss, an artificial *gite* situated at the foot of the *cirque*. Beside it, a spring issued from the ground. Davie had practically lived up there at one point in his life, but it did not seem as if it were ever used, now.

So up and on, past the past. Up the scree to the base of the North Peak baking in the sun, as the South Peak lay in deep shadow, like the Towers guarding the Land of Mordor. To our surprise, a couple had beat us to it. A rather surly lad, clanking with gear and busy with rope, and a nymphet sunning herself on the rocks like a female Pan. She was lovely: long golden hair played with by the sun, blue eyes, and an athletic body that her stripey pants and T-shirt emphasised. She smiled, her partner scowled. We two new arrivals said nothing, but watched them move off.

The nymphet soon followed her partner up the first pitch, a slabby wall with small balance holds reaching a grassy ledge. While Davie and I were roping up we watched the nymphet's partner disappear round a corner.

'We'll no need a belay here, it's jist a stroll,' said Davie, and shot off leaving me startled and still girding my loins. He reached the ledge beside the nymphet in seconds. There, on the right stance, he attached himself to her belay. From below as I moved up the wall I could hear, in between the deep tones of Davie, the sweet tinkle of her laugh. For the first time I wished I did not let Davie do all the leading.

For the rest of the climb Davie always contrived to arrive at the nymphet's belay just as her partner was leaving — looking ever more surly as he did so. He was probably used to such objective hazards in his climbing career. But Davie timed his moves to perfection; it struck me that I had never seen him move so confidently. He thus arrived at the halfway terrace to recline beside the nymphet on an ample, soft couch, just as her leader was grappling with the crux ahead.

'Jist stay doon there,' came from above. 'There's nae mair room on the terrace.'

The two on the ledge were getting on famously, while the first and last on the route were becoming increasingly frustrated and annoyed.

I reached the terrace and managed the crux surprisingly easily: an exposed crack, ascended by jamming — and by not looking at the exposure. I thought I might name it nymphet's crack in honour of the ascent. But then in a cave pitch above, all sight and sense of the others was lost. I shouted up for instructions; but sound was obviously not carrying up, though it did so, weakly, down. Murmurings and sweet laughter could be heard indistinctly from above. I bawled, 'Could ye stop yer cinoodlin, and gie me a ticht rope!' but might as well have spoken to myself.

With trepidation I emerged from the cave and hauled myself over a boulder. Above me sat Davie, with a saft daft look on his face which changed to surprise: 'ye didnae say ye were climbing. I've telt ye, aye shout "Climbing"! That could be dangerous.'

He tut-tutted and the nymphet smiled approvingly at his skill. I decided there was no point saying anything. We all finished the route soon after.

At the top Davie suggested to his morose fellow-leader that Ramshead Wall made a good finish to the route, taking you directly onto the summit. A fine steep wall on good holds. The gruff leader, doubtless to avoid losing face, did as suggested followed by his lady.

'Could we nae jist walk roon tae the top?' I asked in a bit of a bad mood, feeling neglected.

'I tell ye man, the view this wye is better,' replied Davie, look-ing directly up the wall. My eyes followed his. Blue sky, fluffy clouds, a light breeze. Vertical quartzite rock, glistening. And smooth rounded contours, gentle protuberances. Poetry in motion, in stripey pants and T-shirt.

Later in the pool by the dam, cooling our sunburn in the water, we cooled our nostalgia, regret and jealousy in words. Davie was floating wearing only his sun cap. Taes and willie bobbing in the water, he mused: 'I think I'm in love. She was delightful. Her hair, it kept blowing intae my face on the belays. I couldnae concentrate . . .'

'I noticed.'

Then after a while, cooled down a little, he added: 'ah, but she'll be just like the rest. When she's got that lad signed sealed and delivered, it'll be nae mair beets and belays, but engagements, dream houses, weans. It reminds me o' the time I was in . . .'

I dived under the water, and missed what came next. I had to dive a few times but do not think I missed anything new.

BEFORE A FALL

We were looking for a little practice ice work, in preparation for a trip to the Austrian glaciers in the Alps. It had been a mild winter, but snow in March had at last given us the opportunity to don crampons and wield ice axes. Looking for something a bit different, we decided on a trip to Gorton bothy and a gully ascent next day of Beinn a' Chreachain. Davie was bit uncertain about this obscure mount, but relented on it being pointed out that no less than J.H.B. Bell had thought it worthy of his attentions. I was reassured by the fact that the great man had pronounced it 'steep but not difficult'. We thought to copy his ascent and traverse of the tops between Gorton and Bridge of Orchy, a fine winter day's walking.

Gorton is an old shepherd's cottage a few miles off the road which crosses Rannoch Moor to Glencoe. The night walk in took place under a sky full of stars, and enough moon to discern the outlines of the shaggy Scots pines of Crannach Wood as we ascended the glen. The late train to Fort William cut through the darkness beyond the wood as we walked. Formerly it had to halt at Gorton siding to take on water and fuel before continuing its journey; the ruins of the siding master's cottage can still be seen from the train as it hurries by without stopping. So too did we, fighting against the gathering frost to keep warm, hurrying over the unyielding ground. Prospects for the next day seemed excellent, and we reached the bothy in good time and high spirits.

There was light inside. We halted at the door, making enough noise to warn of our arrival, and then crossed the threshold. A weak flame flickered in the grate, and a sleeping bag was stretched before the fire. From inside it, a bearded head with gentle eyes stared at the new arrivals.

'Fine night,' Davie offered as an opening.

The figure made no reply, or at least no audible one, and we went about our business.

64

'Ye dinna mind if we cook?'

This time an audible assent to the proposal was gained, and we took possession of the table to prepare a meal. On the table lay a sketch pad, with pen and crayon drawings: of mountains. Flicking through them, Davie queried, 'are these your drawings? They're good!'

The artist claimed them, and explained that he wandered the bothies, making drawings. Then on his return home to Manchester, where he was on the dole, he translated the drawings into oil paintings, when he could scrape up enough money for the paint. Another hobo of Thatcherism, I thought.

'Do you sell them?' I asked.

He explained that he had not tried to. We offered to buy a painting each, and chose drawings from the book: Davie the fine prow of Beinn Achaladair through Crannach Wood, I the corrie we were to climb in the next day. The artist seemed astonished, delighted, and took our names and addresses eagerly. He looked at the drawings again, as if for the first time.

'I'll have to charge you a lot: maybe fifty pounds,' he hesitantly offered.

'A mere bagatelle for the members o' the Stobcross Gentlemen's Climbing Club,' reassured Davie. 'Ye've tae be o' independent means tae jine.'

Morning showed cloud. Cloud so low we could hear, but not see, the morning train to Fort William, which ran here near the bothy before crossing the moor. The artist lay in his sleeping bag waiting for us to depart. As he watched our preparations, he appeared impressed that we intended to climb a mountain.

'I never go high,' he said. 'I don't feel safe.'

'Aye, weel, ye've tae know what ye're daeing,' agreed Davie.

'Have you ever had an accident?'

'Just the ance, fan I fell in a burn,' I joked.

But having said it, I wished I had not. It seemed a tempting of fate.

After farewells and reminders about the paintings, we headed off. Across the river, across the railway track. Hoping that the mist would rise. And rise it did, so that by the time we reached the corrie of Beinn a' Chreachain, the pouting lip of the cornice was visible far above. We sat in a landscape of snowbridges over burns full with melt, and ate before the ascent.

'Ye think the lad will come up wi' the picters?' I asked.

'Ye nivver know. Though I wish he'd done some o' the Ben or the Buachaille. I mean, dae ye really want tae remember these daft hills aboot here?'

I was looking upwards as Davie spoke, and at his words it seemed as if the sulk of the cornice lip stiffened to a sneer below the heavy brow of cloud.

'Aye, it's nae likely tae be a memorable day at this rate, wi' the weather an a'.'

The snow was soft at the bottom of the gully, ideal for step kicking, and the headwall seemed very easy angled. We decided crampons were not necessary. After we had kicked up a couple of hundred feet, the slope steepened.

'Didnae look this steep fae doon below,' I observed.

The snow had now changed character. The soft covering had thinned to a couple of powdery inches on top of old hard snow, verging on ice.

'Time tae get the crampons on,' said Davie.

We cut sitting platforms in the snow, then strapped on the extra footwear. This helped. Though the snow gave no purchase, and balled up under our feet, we could give the crampons a bite in the hard snow by scraping away the soft stuff with our axes. We progressed cautiously for another three hundred feet or so in this manner. We turned a rocky fin dividing the gully on the left. After this, it steepened further, to the short headwall below the cornice and the summit plateau. We cut big steps to increase security, till we were directly under the cornice at the foot of the short headwall. The cornice curled glistening above us, silently.

I moved to the side and waited as Davie kicked his way up the short wall. Then he reached with his ice axe over the thinnest part of the cornice lip to pull himself to safety. He seemed poised, frozen in mid-air. Except for his head, slowly turning to look at me. It said, 'WE'RE DEAD!'

The headwall had come away.

And then he was moving, on a detached block of snow which was veering towards me. Just before impact the ground on which I stood moved off too, in a huge slab, and I was falling.

Falling, tumbling, falling. And with my head, my unprotected head, below my feet. No fear, no feeling at all, only the sensation of incredible velocity. And the desire to right myself before reaching the fin of rock at the gully junction. The image of an egg smashing on a wall passed into my mind and stayed there.

I could see patches of blue sky, black rock, white snow whirling with great rapidity overhead, like a speeded-up film. Not much snow could have come adrift; I was aware I was not being buried. The axe was still in my hands, both hands. I lashed out with it, trying to catch the hard snow, to right myself. The point impacted. My lower body flew past my weakly anchored upper torso, and I was looking down through my feet. But the axe hold gave way, and I was again accelerating towards that rib of rock, seen now below me. I realised I had not come far in the recent forever.

And then I was flying in mid-air, over the rib of rock, hurled until I crashed down on my back, heading again for the rock debris at the lochanside.

But I was slowing down now. Axe scratching a deceleration from the hard snow, heels taking the edge off velocity. Slowing down. My head was not smashed. The avalanche debris was left behind; I would not be buried. Injured or not, I was slowly aware that I would not die. Suddenly my heart started pounding, and I was gasping for breath. With fear, with panic.

Stopped, I looked at the loch below. For a long time. There was no pain, but I hesitated to move or turn in case motion revealed some damage. Then I remembered Davie for the first time, and looked back up the gully, six hundred feet to where the headwall had broken like the wax running down a candle.

Halfway to the summit was a black speck, impossible to identify at that distance. It was not moving. I called, and there was no answer. After replacing a crampon that had been partly wrenched off in the fall, I retraced that fall in reverse, calling out all the time. I was hoping for, but half not expecting, an answer.

The speck was a body, was Davie; that was clear as I approached. When I came up, he spoke.

'I think I've hurt my stomach wi' my axe.'

Of the axe, lost in the fall, there was no sign.

'Can ye walk?'

'I think so.'

'Gies yer pack, and tak my axe as a walkin stick.'

It was four hundred feet to the loch, then four miles to the car. It took us six hours.

The injured man would not hear of a rescue operation.

'I'll be a' right, I'll see the doctor when I get haim. Of course I'll be able to drive. They'll laugh at us for getting the rescue for some wee dunt. And imagine, on a daft hill naebody's heard o'! Rescued fae the Buachaille wid be bad enough, but here!'

I knew there was no point in arguing. I was annoyed but at the same time reassured by his response, which was in character.

We crawled down from the corrie, through the pine woods, no eye for their beauty now. The casualty had occasional stabs of severe pain, but could walk. I was in a state of euphoria, exulting in the fact that I was still alive, had years to live, when I found myself alone, deep in the wood. I had wandered off from Davie, forgotten about him. I ran back in panic to find him sitting on a log, resting. I shouldered both packs again, and took it slower, fearing I was suffering from shock.

We reached the railway; he complained of cold. I took his spare clothes from his rucksack and began dressing him anew. Opening his damp shirt, I exposed the wound. I saw the reaction on his face to what passed over mine. He did not look down, but asked, 'whit is it?'

A gash across his stomach, deep and clean to the livid, glistening insides, had been made by the axe. There was no blood.

'Ye've a wee cut, Davie. I think ye should get intae yer sleeping bag, and I'll get the rescue.'

'They'll laugh at us. I've aye got myself aff a hill. Keep changing the clothes.'

I covered the wound with a dressing to keep it clean. It seemed an inadequate ministration, but the only other thing I had was painkillers, and I recalled that these should not be given to people with stomach wounds.

Along the railway line. Along the Land Rover track. Slowly. The farm was in sight for an eternity before we reached it. At the car I tried again.

'I'm gyan tae phone for an ambulance.'

'No! I'll drive myself haim!' persisted the injured man.

Luckily some people were passing, and I hailed them for moral support. They forced the protesting climber into the farm, where he finally collapsed in agony and resisted no more. While he was sped towards hospital later in the ambulance, I sat by a roaring fire, plied with whisky, high on the loss of responsibility. By the end of the evening, I had practically carried Davie, as well as his pack, down off the mountain.

When the morphine wore off next day, Davie was told he had punctured his colon and was lucky to have avoided septicaemia.

We went back for the ice axe, a fine old Aschenbrenner that Davie thought had a few more years left in it, once he was out of hospital. And we found it, a little rusted, where the snow covering it had melted, before we traversed our tops back to the farm again. He used the axe in the Alps three months later. It was a little while before the fall haunted me, every time I set foot on snow. It still does.

The lad with the pictures never appeared.

'Maybe jist as weel,' Davie would say. 'Ye wouldnae want a reminder o' yon. These daft hills are nae safe. It's aye there that accidents happen.'

And he still thinks he would probably have been all right driving home.

TRENCH WARFARE

It was November. It was raining, and miserable. Normal bothy weather, in fact. So we sought out a new howff where we had never before ventured. I had just heard a radio programme about an old woman in Fort William, who had been born in Glen Pean. She told tales of landslides in the narrow defile that was the glen, and of walking out for the train at Glenfinnan to go shopping in the Fort. So Glen Pean bothy it would be.

Neither of us had a recent map of the area.

'We'll need tae buy ane,' I innocently ventured.

'Buy wan!' stormed Davie. 'Nonsense. I've an auld 1" that covers maist o' the terrain. These new stereophonic three-dimensional maps, wi' their fancy contours in metres, ye cannae read them. And the distances are much further in centimetres, than in inches. A nice wee walk the size o' yer thumb, it's the length o' yer haund on these new maps.'

I know I should have persisted, but I did not. So it was off with an O.S. work of art, cloth set and, I noticed as Davie hit the bumps on the Loch Arkaig road in a fashion intended to send the 2CV into orbit, 'last revised in 1952'. I mentioned this, casually.

'But the geology's jist the same. Or dae ye think that glacial drift has had a major impact in the last third o' a century?'

'But . . .'

'But naethin. Save yer breath for the walk in.'

Sound advice, as it turned out.

We arrived at the road end in mirk dark, in the middle of a downpour that did not abate till we reached the bothy much later. On went the headtorches and the waterproofs. Teeth were gritted and off we trudged to the river flowing out of Glen Dessary. We could hear its roar before we saw its white boil against the black night. Davie got the map out.

'The brig is doon there, beside the hoose, according tae this map, and then the path follaes the river right tae the bothy.'

I studied the map and agreed with his analysis: nothing could be simpler than finding our howff. But just ahead of us, upriver from the marked bridge, was a stout new construction arching across the torrent. The same thought was crossing both our minds.

'Let's see though, whaur this ane goes, first.'

We crossed the river and came to a Forestry fence, behind which we could discern the dark waving outlines of trees against the sky.

'A plantation. It's no' on the map.' Davie sounded annoyed, as if the trees were committing a trespass by being there. Which they were in a sense: desecrating another Highland glen with monocultural tax evasion. But this was no time for such thoughts.

'Question is,' he continued, 'whaur does the path go?'

We thought awhile in the downpour. I said it first.

'It could ging onywye. Let's stick tae the ither path. At least we ken it's there, and it leads tae the bothy.'

Unfortunately, Davie agreed with me for once.

We dropped down to the abandoned farmhouse, and passed its rickle of outbuildings, gaining again the river's edge. The rain and darkness seemed to have abated a little, or possibly our eyes were just becoming adjusted to the conditions. For we found the bridge quickly. Or what was left of it. A quartet of wires, low slung, and with a few loose and rotting boards over the bottom wires. Davie went first, cautiously. I came after, in fear and trembling.

'At least ye couldnae see muckle,' was my relieved comment.

'That's the worst o'er,' came from my cheery companion. 'Look, there's the path gaun doon by, and it's gettin lighter.'

And indeed, at first it was a splendid path, dropping to the junction of the rivers flowing out of Glens Pean and Dessary and then heading up the former, keeping to the river bank just as the cloth antique in Davie's pooch indicated. To our right was the fence of the new plantation; to our left by the river, some real trees: birch, rowan, oak.

And soon we came to another bridge. Davie consulted his map. 'We dinnae cross,' he said, 'jist keep tae the north side o' the river.'

At this point the plantation appeared to come very close to the river, hardly leaving space to edge along between the overtowering fence and the river in spate. The river has risen here, I thought, and obliterated part of the path: we will pick it up again further along. So, packs threatening to peel us off backwards into the river, we mounted the fence and started on a girdle traverse of its structure, hoping to regain the path in due course. The fence wobbled, we threatened to topple over. So we climbed over and tried inside. Here we crashed through sodden branches, slapping our faces with stinging needles; then stumbled and fell in drainage ditches, which brought the water above our knees.

Then the fence appeared to retreat a little from the water's edge, so we crossed back over again. There was still no path, but at least some treeless terrain to walk on. Till we came to a burn. It did not look very deep, so I stepped in and started crossing, holding onto the bottom of the fence for balance. Ankles sank, followed by knees, and then when it got waist high I panicked, and started trying to climb up the swaying fence. It buckled beneath my weight, but allowed a traverse to be effected, feet splashing around in the water. Davie learned from my mistake, and traversed the fence above the water line.

We sat drookit and peching on the other bank for a while.

'Ye ken fit I think?' I queried.

'Aye,' said Davie. 'They've dug up the path for the forestry; there's nae path.'

I appended my silent assent to this analysis, and thought of the miles ahead.

It continued, unrelenting, whiles in the river, whiles in the plantation, whiles on a sliver of bank for several slow hours. But finally a dyke told us the bothy was at hand, and a light guided our way to its door. Feeling like a couple of survivors from the Battle of the Somme, we crossed the portals. There was a party in possession. As we cascaded water on entry, they looked at us. Unwelcomingly it seemed.

'That was a hellish path,' I offered.

There was silence for a while as they surveyed us, covered in glaur. Finally one said, 'we thought it was quite a good path.'

Davie gave them one of his choicest foul looks, and later commented as we set out our wee dookit, 'some folk are aye boasting. Either that, or they were being damned cheeky.'

I could only agree. Even with the river lower, and in daylight, that was a rough ride to any bothy in my opinion. This encounter set the tone for the weekend. The other party repaired upstairs, leaving us to take possession of the lower quarters.

We bedded quickly, and rose with the grey dawn. Outside it had not improved. We breakfasted in our sleeping bags, hesitating to put on our wet clothes again and make a sortie out. When we finally did, the cloud greeted us low down on the hills, and there was a drizzle. But it was a long way to come and do nothing, so we reluctantly donned our garments and set off into the depths of Glen Pean to look for a river crossing. Glen Pean is the narrowest and possibly the steepest glen in Scotland; hence the problems with landslides. That day we had a different problem. There was simply nowhere for the water to go, so it filled up the glen, and the river became a loch. After a mile we came to a beetling crag, to whose base the water had reached. It was impassible, the path under several feet of water. So we must needs ascend the hillside for almost 1,000 feet to gain the upper reaches of the glen. Not a good start.

We squelched on past Lochan Leum an-t-Sagairt looking for the crossing that would take us to the slopes of Sgurr nan Coireachan, but found never the one. Further on, below Coire a Beithe, amidst a jumble of boulders by a tiny lochan set in a thick copse of birches, we sat down and ate. Overhead was grey, but below us lay a sodden spilled mint of spangled birch coins, fallen from the trees.

'Yon Bonnie Prince Charlie couldnae hae been sic a saftie if he came through here,' was Davie's philosophical preprandial tit-bit. He then got out his by now sodden map and added: 'There's a stalkers' path marked at the end o' this wid. If it's there, we tak it; if no, I vote we retreat.'

Others obviously had designs on the stalkers' path, for a couple of the party from the bothy now arrived. Though not in any way competitive, Davie regards it as bad form to be overtaken, so I prepared to move.

'Haud on,' he said. 'Let them past.'

I must have looked quizzical, for he added, 'there'll be snaw. Let them find and brak a trail. If it disappears o'er an edge, we'll turn back.'

So we nodded to the young lads as they powered past us, wishing them luck. They did not reply, possibly having worked out the motive for our long lunch break.

The path saved the day. Without it, it would have been impossible to find the ridge in the thick mist. Once on it, however, it was impossible to lose direction, except by falling off the ridge. And this the lads whose footsteps we followed had managed to avoid doing. It was a hard fight along to Sgurr Thuilm, through knee-deep snow, and against a thumping wind. We said little, saw nothing but each other, did not stop till the way ahead lay downhill. These lads had followed an outlier of the ridge that pointed back towards Strathan, where our car was, and we followed.

Here the solid mist began to break a little, the wind whipped at us suddenly a little more wildly, and it was clearing. Through fragments of cloud we saw the symmetrical prow of Streap loom through the broken mist like a knife. Glimpses of the ridge we had blindly crossed were soon given to us. A shaft of light hit Streap as though directing onlookers to marvel. This I was doing, when Davie commented, 'how dae we get back across that river?'

I had not thought of that, and it dampened my interest in nature a little. We could not ford the river in spate conditions. So it was either a repeat of last night's trench warfare, or back to the birch wood at the head of the glen where we had crossed earlier in the day. We descended further, pondering the alternatives.

All the way down, it was clearing around us. Peaks were coming shining out of the mist, glistening against the spreading blue of the sky. Davie suddenly let out a cry of delight — clearly nature was having a profound impact on his sensitive soul. He has forgotten the rigours ahead, I thought.

'Look!' he cried, pointing towards Strathan.

I looked, and realised the material basis of his joy. From the old farm, starting from the new bridge we had rejected in the night, a Land Rover track cut through the plantation to within a mile of the bothy. There was no need to repeat the battle of yesterday's dreadful night. A quick return and a roaring fire were anticipated. We got the former, but not the latter.

I began to have my doubts when collecting the sodden wood.

'Davie, this is sae weet, I'm leaving thoomb prints in it.'

'Listen, I've never failed tae get a fire tae light yet. Ye've jist tae follae the auld Sheshone method that I learned in Wyoming, and ye cannae fail.'

'But this Glen Pean, nae Indian country.'

He was not to be discouraged, and built an edifice in the lum that looked as if it were intended to send smoke signals across the Atlantic. But more than Indian magic was needed this time. After a couple of hours it still looked like a charcoal burner's furnace, smouldering away and giving out much smoke, but little heat. Davie was downcast.

'I've nivver, NIVVER failed afore, tae light a fire.'

He was not cheered up either by a series of cheeky comments from our companions in the bothy. They first asked us why we had taken so long on the ridge, and then cast jocular aspersions on our fire-lighting abilities. We retired to our sleeping bags, fuming in mind and frozen in body. I got to sleep counting the witty one-liners I should have though up in reply to the baiting.

In the morning we were still abed when our fellows prepared to leave. We were glad to see the back of them, for we had not really hit it off. We were hoping they would go and leave us to have a leisurely Sunday breakfast in peace. However, they were having a confab at the door, and then one of them came into our corner of the bothy and asked, 'you came in by the path down by the river. We thought we might go back that way, what's it like?'

Surprise. Temptation. We lay silent awhile, communicating telepathically. Then Davie spoke.

'Weel, it IS a bit rougher than the Land Rover track, but it should hae dried oot a bit by now. And it's really lovely doon by the river. If ye're no in a hurry, I recommend it.'

We waited a little, then rushed to the window. Sure enough, the conscripts were heading for the trenches.

'Let's get doon the road,' I said. 'They'll probably let doon wir tyres fan they find oot fit the path's like.'

But we had our breakfast in peace, ambled out to the car, and still there was no sign of the other party.

'I wonder whit's keepin them?' chortled Davie.

HOHENWEG

Coming down out of the clouds, we knew we didn't want to die. We saw the fields and trees below, hoped the descent would be uneventful after the bomb scare and search at Birmingham. Two of us. One never before in the Alps, one not there for fifteen years.

We achieved a safe, level landing, and waited for the ruck-sacks at the baggage lounge. These made a sad contrast to the Gucci suitcases and designer luggage.

'It's time we got some new gear.'

'Nonsense. That pack is only 20 years old; there's another 20 years' wear left in it.'

'Maybe, but is there 20 years' wear left in us?'

*

Kaunergrathutte.

We are in an A.A.C. Hut, below the Watzmann Mountain. The hut was a favourite of Hermann Buhl, of Nanga Parbat fame; we can look across to Buhl's Pillar, one of his climbs, from the hut. It's a Grade 5; we won't be doing it.

The first thing I noticed, in innocence, is that the mountains here are big, huge to me. The second is that they are steep from the valley floor; I'll never complain about the walk to a Scottish hill again. The hut is at about 7,500 feet, 4,000 from the valley floor. It took us nearly four hours. First through steep forest, scarred by landslips, then a gentle alp covered with flowers and alpine rhododendrons, then steep again through moraines and the first patches of snow.

When we arrived Davie collapsed on a bench outside the hut. An Alsatian growled at him, then a crusty old guide did the same; he was sitting on the 'Fuhrerbank', the warden's seat. He moved off, grumbling.

'I don't like all this Fuhrer stuff. Nae wonder they've jist voted in Waldheim, since they've fun' oot he was a Nazi.'

But once they discovered we were Scottish, they seemed quite tickled to have us. It's a bit like an S.M.C. hut in standard, but they do all the cooking for you. Bergsteigeressen, plates of pasta.

19th.

Our first day here will be an enforced rest and acclimatisation day. The weather is a bit like Glencoe in January, a bad day. The mist is right down, it is very cold and trying to sleet.

Spent the day reading old Alpine magazines, huddled round the fire in the stove. People are sitting around dubbining boots, except for a party listening to uplifting lectures on technique from a guide. Getting here was an achievement for me, and I feel I could doze cosily for the fortnight. But I suppose we'll get a chance to try to fulfil my modest ambitions.

20th.

Another appalling day; we've been clagged up 36 hours, and not even seen any of the peaks nearby. Davie has got cabin fever, and descended 4,000 feet to the valley to get some supplies for the hill. Another day of this and inertia could take over.

There are parties here with guides who seem to go out in all weathers, though they can see bugger all. The unguided lounge about the hut, harassed by an old grumpy fellow rattling ice screws. His official position appears to be vague, and he mutters that in his day, everyone went up the mountain.

Davie returned from the valley. All the shops had been closed: it was the local half day.

21st.

Sun and shadow at 6 a.m. Blue skies, a beautiful Alpine day. The glare, brightness here is dazzling.

The Watzmann is a fearful monster with smashed ridges and huge icefalls. We decided on Schwabenkopf, an easier ascent approached through a high moraine and then a snowfield, which made easy going in the sun. We ascended up to a high col whence we could see the next valley, the next range. Here, instead of saying that's Ross-shire, that's Inverness-shire, you say: that's Switzerland, that's Italy. It had been hot but enjoyable work, and we lunched at the col.

A shattered arete snaked ahead of us. It proved technically quite easy, though fearfully exposed on our right. And the rock was poor. Davie did not lose the chance to praise Scottish rock, adding, 'there should be a sign, "Please replace the holds after use".'

We reached the top in guidebook time, to see the real top about half a mile away along a twisting, Cuillin-like ridge reached by traversing a sloping slab over a big drop. We finally stood on the top at midday; my first 'Dreitausander'.

At the col we joined up with another couple of parties, both of whom had given up on the ascent. The descent from the col had become sheet ice, now the sun was down; hard work with axe and crampons, cautious of a slip to the boulders below.

What's been done here must be the ultimate indignity nature can suffer. I suppose it can stand man tilling a few fields and so on, but to tame the mountains with a system of huts, paths, signposts, Seilbahns — this is really adding insult to injury. In some ways it is less wild than Scotland, less of a wilderness.

23rd.
Taschach Haus.

Today we reached the hut we'll be staying at for a few days. A place of amazing luxury, with showers, central heating and self-service restaurant. The original refuge stands outside, looking a bit like a Scottish bothy. Buhl was here too and almost met his end in the Taschach glacier when he fell down a crevasse. To my eyes it is a massive sweep of ice, cut up by crevasses and pillared by seracs; it is also filthy, as all glaciers are, with debris of the mountain.

We came here from the Kaunergrat by a high level pass, the Cottbusser Hohenweg, which contoured the mountains on the western Pizthal at about 6,000 feet. Most of it was along a high, well-formed track. But as we came after an hour to a grassy alp, we met a family, parents and son. The father smiled mysteriously.

'There is a little surprise ahead.'

We didn't ask what it was.

The track suddenly descended about two hundred feet over steeply sloping slabs, which were running with water. A fixed metal rope, looped through pegs, showed the way down. Davie went first. I followed. Then he found the surprise.

'I want my surcharge for maintaining the paths refunded,' he cried. 'The rope ends fifty feet fae the bottom.'

By the time he reached the ground, I had reached the frayed end of the wire rope. The only foot and handholds were the pegs. I stood with the tip of my boot on one, and with a finger threaded through another above. The pegs didn't descend vertically (that way was a big penalty clause), but sloped sideways, pulling me out of balance.

Toes trembling, fingers aching, I moved down to where Davie stood smiling.

'That was a scandal,' he said, 'let's gae back for oor path tax.'

We carried on the path, stopping for lunch on the grass by the Riffelsee, a dark green glacier lake, and watched a group of horses grazing. They were actually the first four-footed animals we'd seen (apart from the Alsatian dogs), and wildlife seems limited. A few choughs and wheatears are all the birds we've seen; lots of nice butterflies though. We were reluctant to leave our resting place, as we had a 180-degree panorama of 10,000 foot peaks, glaciers and rock ridges.

'That's anither Buhl route, Seekogel,' said Davie, 'but the rock is supposed to be very bad.'

Another three hours took us to the Taschach, with views opening of the glacier country, the Weisskam, into which we are headed. This part of the Hohenweg was again simplified by the system of fixed ropes; in place this time. Exposure with security. We rested a little among the orchids and rhodys watching a group of marmots, before descending to the hut. The weather was again great today, and we are getting the mountaineers suntan; white bum, feet, noses and ears.

24th.

A day of utter misery for weather. Gale force winds, hailstones and freezing mist. In the morning it was deceptively sunny, with strands of mist swirling round the hut and fingering up the glacier. But the clouds turned black and soon all hell was let loose, with thunder and rain. Some brave souls had departed early, but soon returned cold and frozen, just as on a Scottish winter's day.

The thunderstorm is stotting off the mountains, and the morning's hail is lying white on the ground outside. After my Bohnensuppe for lunch, I decided to go up and see Davie. He was lying in the dormitory reading Faulkner's "Light in August". Or trying to. The guides, clamped indoors because of the weather, were making the most of their time. On the stairs a student was practising abseiling, while out the open window, into which swirled spindrift, another was being versed in crevasse rescue techniques. Other novices sat round, rapt, while a guide, ice screw in hand, delivered a serious lecture. Davie's eyes had a wild look.

'There must,' he said, 'be a limit tae whit ye can say aboot ice screws! We've hid the politics, the economics, the philosophy, the minerology o' the bloody things, and still he's no finished!'

The guide looked quickly at us. He must have had some English, or simply read our faces, for soon he departed with his charges.

26th.

Today a fine day allowed us to climb the Pitztaler Urkund, at 3,250m. At first it was overcast and so were my spirits as we passed the Totenwand, a rock with mementos for all those killed in this area. There seemed to be a lot of them. The path skirted the Taschach glacier before beginning to ascend. Our plan was to ascend a branch of the glacier to a Joch behind the Urkund, traverse it and descend the rock arete back to the hut.

On beginning the ascent of the steepening slope to the Joch, we stopped to rope up. Davie began to lead off, but almost immediately I heard him curse; a crampon ring had broken, and the crampon was flapping loose on his foot. We had to traverse to the arete, and ascend and descend by the same route, over the rock. This was a bit like Pinnacle Ridge but with more serious exposure. And worse rock. It was again rotten, loose, fragile. When not held by ice, the mountains here are moving heaps of stones. From the top we had views deep into glacier country towards the highest mountain here, the Wildspitze. We quickly descended to sunbathe on a flat rock before regaining the hut.

Here we dumped our packs and went to eat. When we came out we found a cluster of guides around our gear. They pointed at the wooden ice axes, and fingered the canvas rucksacks. Davie's crampons brought gasps of amazement and intense discussion.

28th.

An easy day yesterday, back to the luxury of the Riffelsee Hut, and a walk round the See and sunbathe in the afternoon. We decided against the Wildspitze 'for the want of a crampon ring', as the glacier without crampons would have been impossible.

Today we saw our first signs of transhumance in the local economy; a herd of cattle have appeared at the loch. And we saw a shepherd driving sheep up the mountain at 7,000 feet. The soil is very thin here; even in the valley it is a skin over glacial debris, nothing like the lush growth of Scottish hills. As Davie said, 'the hills will seem awfae wee and awfae green when ye get haim.'

29th.

Today Wurmthaler Kopf. Great weather again, the best of the trip. A few fluffy clouds, sun and a cool breeze on nearing the snowfield. The ascent was a bit like an alpine cliché. Lower pastures by the loch munched by soft-eyed cows; the path rising through a high valley where the sheep grazed among the flowers; big floppy-lugged sheep; and then up through steep gorges to the moraines. Here we saw our first wild animals. Little deer-like creatures, with badgery coloured faces and curled horns; later we discovered they were chamois.

After the moraine the path wandered over a snowfield, which we crossed with great trepidation, to a Joch at about 3,000m. The most logical route seemed up a steep snowfield to the summit, but as this was hard and Davie had no crampons, we decided to cross the snowfield to a rocky arete on the horizon, which also led to the summit. Sadly this arete was the biggest slag heap we had climbed yet. We inched up nervously, cleaning the rock as we moved, each handhold loose, until we made it and were rewarded with a stunning view over to the Weisskam. But the descent was worse, our weight dislodging the rock over the arete. To our left was a steep ice slope, to our right a 1,500-feet drop. The stones we dislodged hit nothing till the bottom. With visible relief, we regained the snowfield.

At the bottom we encountered a large group of elderly climbers, who had stepped a duel carriageway through the snow. They were very pleased that we were from the land of oatcakes, and asked about Scottish mountaineering, mentioning some of the places they had heard of. I indicated that we did not think much of the quality of their rock. One replied (the conversation was in German), 'Aber, dies' sind Ur-Bergen' (young mountains).

Davie's ears pricked up, despite his lack of the lingua franca: 'aye, maybe they're your Bergen, but gie me OOR Bergen ony day!'

And with that inimitable contribution to international understanding, we moved off to our descent.

On the way down we stopped to eat dried apricots and glucose tablets. I mentioned that the group we'd met were

German, like most of the climbers here. Austria was like Scotland, Germany like England. The smaller country had the best mountains, and was consequently swamped by the larger. I wondered if it led to the same resentments.

'I suppose ye'll be able tae tell the difference, wi' yer German. But I notice they a' come awa with this "Berg Heil!" when they pass by. I'm nae sure I'm too keen on that. Sounds a bit fascist tae me.'

29th.

Today we moved to our last hut, the Chemnitzer Hutte, a bit more old-fashioned than the others. Dark-stained panelled walls, gas lighting and a big tin stove against the winter blasts. It also has a Seilbahn for materials. After we descended from Riffelsee we discovered at the foot of the Seilbahn a hut with a telephone in it. It was one of these old contraptions where you have to ca' the haunle to get it to work. We also had to reconnect the battery, which literally gave Davie a shock. I communicated with the custodian, and down, swinging, came the overhead bogey to carry our gear up. Davie was very impressed. So we walked up the steepest slopes on grass I've ever seen, unencumbered by the packs. The hills behind the hut are jagged and rocky, with little snow.

Tomorrow is our last day. I can't say, like Hermann Buhl, that it is not really the mountain I have conquered, but myself. Because I'll never conquer myself; I am too aware of my upper limits, how far I can go as a mountaineer. And he's dead, while I intend to stay alive. What Humble said in "On Scottish Hills" echoes my feelings:

> 'I had an uneasy sense of foreboding, that the homeland hills would lose their attraction after Alpine peaks. Nearing Dumbarton I glimpsed Ben Lomond. My heart sank; it had shrunk in size! What of the Cobbler? Off we went to Arrochar. We traversed three peaks leisurely, lovingly. It was as good a day as I have ever had.' (*On Scottish Hills*)

30th.

Just as I sat down to write, the mountain opposite experienced a huge rock fall; a whole buttress appeared to peel away. The echoes of it are still reverberating round the corrie. These mountains will have settled in about a million years time.

We did a climb today, the Hohe Geige, at 3,490m our biggest yet; but it was quite a short day, and hence the sunbathing. Both

83

of us felt really wabbit this morning and reluctant to start, partly due to tiredness, and partly to hunger's cumulative effect. But we fought the good fight, and gradually our 'Mut' rose. We followed the path to a smashed ridge, which we ascended to the snowfield, crossed it and stepped along the sharp snow ridge to the summit cross. Here our finest view yet, across the whole of the Otzthal Alps. We passed an old couple, about 60, who doggedly plodded on, and eventually returned to the hut after nine hours, twice what we took. The old fellow said to us, 'sie sind wahre Bergsteiger' — rather an exaggerated compliment.

But we ourselves were passed by a Farrah Fawcett blonde, perfectly coiffed, wearing trainers and running shorts, and carrying, as we discovered when we gained the top, only a packet of cigarettes with her. Sweaty, with our khaki shorts and peeling noses, we watched as she displayed her fine legs and lightly clad torso and chain-smoked, tossing her locks in the alpine breeze.

'It's nae fair,' said Davie.

I agreed with the comment, in all its ambiguity.

In the evening a splendid thunderstorm lit up the mountains all around us, forked lightning flashing from peak to peak. We stood watching it till it passed away.

Davie broke the silence.

'Aye, ye didnae dae too bad. Four Dreitausander.'

After a pause he continued: 'd'ye think onybody at haim would buy a used Otztwal Alps kit? A thirty-year-auld guidebook, a couple o' maps, and an unused token for the Taschach Haus shower thrown in?'

On the way back we whiled away the time by visiting the Alpine Museum at Innsbruck, since we got in free with our Austrian Alpine Club membership. I found Davie staring at an inter-war exhibit case with rapt attention.

'Nae wonder thae guides were impressed by oor stuff. Look, there's my crampons . . . and your ice axe! We'll haud on tae oor gear, it could be valuable wan day.'

THE YOUNG TEAM: AN EPIC

There were three of them, mates, and invariably seen together. With their Yuppie haircuts and attire, they even looked alike, and it was difficult to tell them apart. Especially as their names were Bobby, Lobbie and Dobbie, or Benny, Kenny and Lennie, or something. So it was easy to get them mixed up, and when you shouted at one, and got angry when he did not reply, and then discovered that it was another one you wanted, this made you angrier. Really, though, they were nice fellas, well behaved and respectful, and what's more they showed promise. Acolytes at last?

It is true that they were much given to multi-coloured stretch-pants, as worn by circus clowns and rock athletes. And they drank stuff with funny names that smelt like you should slap it under your oxters before going to the dancing — or discos as they would have it — spurning the Good Lord's Christian Water of Life. But they did seem to think that there might be more to life than the Finnieston Wall. And once they had got a whiff of the total mountain experience on the Whangie, they were raring to go. To somewhere with a bit of depth, heavy with history, where men in tweed and tricouni had gone. But something not so hard that their mentors would be out of breath and reduced to silence. And so it was agreed.

'Observatory Ridge,' said Davie. 'A real mountain experience. A century o' history laid oot before you, graven on tablets of stone. And funny enough, I've never actually done it. That should be a splendid day out for the young lads!'

The travel logistics, complicated as they were, were the simplest part. One of the mates would accompany the mature duo in the car, while the other two would get the train to Fort William. Of course, they got their timetables wrong, and caught the Oban train, eventually arriving in Fort Bill at midnight. In borrowed bendy boots they trudged through the Everglades behind the Distillery towards base camp on the old narrow-

gauge railway that skirts the Ben. There they crawled into their
see-through sleeping bags to shiver the night away.

'It's a wonder yer mammies let ye oot,' scolded Davie, from
the depths of a bag that looked as if its making had threatened
the continued existence of the world's eider duck population.

Things had not promised well: thick mist all day, which had
turned to drizzle as we bedded down. Next day looked like
being one of those two days in three when the Ben declines to
show its face to the sun. A 6 a.m. trip out to relieve the bladder
of Guinness confirmed that the dawn was failing to fight its way
through the incubus. But at 7 a.m. another hopeful announced
that the mist was lifting, rolling back up the hill like a carpet. As
we watched, first the zig-zags to the dam, and then the foot of
the cliff, were visible below the curtain of the mist.

'What'll we do?' asked one of the mates.

'Ye've got tae gie the hill a chance,' were the oracular words
uttered with finality.

Minds turned to the preparation of breakfast. Of course,
barring a few sandwiches and a packet of biscuits, the mates
had enough for a church mouse between them.

'Nae wonder yer hair grows that funny wye,' was all they got
from the gentlemen eating kippers and porridge at their leisure.
'Dr. Bell would hae barred ye fae the Ben for sic a breakfast.'

Eventually we started off for the mighty Ben: men, two ropes
and a wealth of ironmongery, mostly belonging to the younger
generation, and including many new-fangled things that Davie
eyed with suspicion. A 'friend':

'That'll get ye intae trouble in places ye shouldnae be.'

A 'betta-brake':

'That'll jist encourage a leader fa'.'

A 'descendeur':

'Is that no awfae defeatist?'

And so forth, in similar vein, as we squelched through the
mud of the path to reach the C.I.C. hut a couple of hours out
from the camp. We had a break for nourishment and water,
while Davie plied eager ears with tales of Bell, MacPhee and
Kellet, whose routes were recounted with awe.

'Mak ye feart jist tae read about Kellet's routes, far less dae
them.'

The mist had risen halfway up Tower Ridge, revealing the top
of the Douglas Boulder; the lower section of Carn Dearg Buttress
appeared, and Kenny reached for the support of the C.I.C. hut
as the lines of Sassenach and Centurion were traced. The mates

were clearly awed at the scale, almost Alpine, of what was
revealed, and of what lay hidden.

'Aye, whaur's yer Auchinstarry Quarry noo? I've been up
here on a simmer's day, and seen naebody, naebody. Yet doon
at that Polldubh, there's standing room only for the rock gym-
nasts. It's a disgrace, a disgrace!'

Appetites whetted, we continued up to the foot of Tower
Ridge. Just at the beginning of the Douglas Boulder, blue gaps
appeared in the sky, and the half-raised curtain of mist was
pulled fully back to reveal the splendour of the set. Over a mile
of cliff: buttresses, ridges and gullies rising for nearly 2,000 feet
above.

'Jist think whit the pioneers thocht when they saw that. Their
eyes picked oot the ridges first. Collie did Tower Ridge, and
Raeburn, a man thirty years ahead o' his time, did the first
ascent o' Observatory, that ye can see there.'

He pointed a little further up the mountain to where a ridge,
steeper than Tower, but less well defined at the top, rose black
and inviting. By now the weather gave us no option but to go
ahead, and we scrambled past the debris of earthenware pots
thrown over Gardyloo Gully by the original inhabitants of the
Observatory which gave the Ridge its name.

We divided into two parties, and decided that the duo (Benny
and Kenny) should go first, as three would be slower on the
rope. The first party intended to catch the last train from the
Fort back to Glasgow, and it was assumed they would 'burn
off' their slower companions. The climb normally takes about
three hours in summer, but that conditions were not normal was
obvious from the big greasy slab that sloped away above us: the
rock was running with water.

The first man to go was Benny, who indicated that it was a
bit slippy as he ran out in his sticky boots to a distant, unseen
belay. His second, Kenny, confirmed this by slithering down
like a fish on a slab the first three times he tried to get off the
ground. Finally a mixture of tight rope from above, and the
volume of imprecations from below, led to his disappearing
round a corner on the horizon. His detractors however soon
found that his slow start had had a cause in the water which
caused feet to slither, and fingers to freeze into numbness.

'I hope the sun dries the rock when it gets higher,' said
Bobby, who was partnering Davie and myself.

'It'll tak a' day tae dry, even in the sun,' observed Davie, with
a slightly worried look.

We expected to find the belay stance vacant above, as the advance party sped ahead. But there was Kenny, the hindmost looking abandoned even by the Devil, and he was shouting 'tight rope!' every time he moved more than an inch off the ground. When he finally did move, pulling himself up, holding onto the rope and splayed across the rock, he asked, 'where does the route go? Does it follow the marks on the rock?'

'Of course it does, ye expletive bastard, where dae ye think it would go?' bawled Davie.

Progress was inordinately slow, and the second party had plenty of time to watch the armies of ant-like figures ascending Tower Ridge with great speed. Time too for a history lesson in stone from Davie.

'Thae auld-timers did these routes when they were hard. Hemp rope, and nae protection. And now look at the future o' Scottish mountaineering!'

He jerked a finger towards the advance party. Kenny was meanwhile grappling with a steep wall above a spike on which he stood. I saw the train, miles below, heading towards Glasgow.

'There's yer train, Kenny and Benny!' I remarked.

'Eh, where?' asked Kenny, turning to look. As he turned, he promptly peeled off, yelping for help. His leader held him, legs flailing in the air inches above Davie's expostulating head. After Kenny righted himself, the history lesson was continued through the Gude Buke.

'But Raeburn jist took three hours for the first ascent o' Observatory. At this rate we'll nae be up by dark. It's becoming an epic.'

'But Raeburn had an advantage; he didnae hae Kenny wi' him,' I suggested.

On and on it went. At one pitch, as third man in the second party, I noticed that as I advanced the rope remained slack. My partners were out of sight and sound, and I advanced, coiling the rope over my shoulder as I went. On reaching the belay stance I found Davie cosily ensconsed above a vertical drop, snoozing in the sunshine, while Bobby, supposedly belaying, was watching the gyrations of Kenny far above with rapt attention.

'I think this is yours,' I said, handing Bobby the rope.

As we went on, accompanied by incessant appeals for a tight rope, and the shower of debris from flapping feet, progress was easier as the rock slowly dried out. Finally we gained the summit, and strolled over to the Observatory ruins to coil the ropes. A snow bunting hopped about the stones.

'At least that's one thing in common wi' the first ascent; Raeburn saw a snaw bunting tae,' I informed them.

'Seven hours, seven hours,' muttered Davie in disbelief. 'That must be an all-time record. Is this whit I've come tae, me that wouldnae dirty my hands on onything less than severe. Me that's done Green Gully, Italian Climb and the like. And you're supposed tae be the Young Team. Seven hours!'

Kenny seemed dazed, semi-comatose. His companions looked at him in wordless amazement as he asked, 'how many megatons do you think it would take to blow up Ben Nevis?'

'Nivver mind that, it's six o'clock, let's get aff this mountain.'

For poor Kenny, the worst was not over. His feet, in borrowed boots, burst into a bleeding agony as he descended to Meall an t-Suidhe, and he staggered across the moor in the darkness more dead than alive.

'You young yins, ye buy a' the fancy gear and the stripey ropes, but ye'll no buy the basic thing: a pair o' beets that will fit ye,' was all the sympathy he got.

Relentlessly we descended, finally crashing through the thicket to the tent, which was found in the pitch blackness more by accident than design. Davie and I were to return to the car, to get back to wives and work on the morrow. The younger ones decided to flop into their sleeping bags and go no further, despite dreams on the descent of a fish supper in the Fort.

'Here, ye'll hae tae dae withoot the chips,' I said, as I handed Kenny a tin of sardines.

Bobby, who had endured the whole day without a murmur, fired his parting shot.

'There are some days that are enjoyable, but that wasnae wan.'

Davie was piqued.

'Oh, come on. That was a total mountain experience, a day tae remember.'

Confirmation came from an unexpected quarter.

'Aye,' said Kenny, 'that was great. Mind and let me know if you're going tae Skye next month.'

Davie and I exchanged looks. But he came.

'He's the last wan we've got,' Davie would say. 'We had three, bit the ither two had some imagination.'

And Kenny would smile. But he still has not bought the boots.

FORCAN TERRIBLE

Davie was at it again. Telling me, half seriously, half jokingly, about how lucky I was to know him. About all the places he had taken me safely, and back again. About his selflessness in guiding me up the classic V.Diffs, when he could have been off somewhere, scrambling over the hard severes.

'And soloing the E6's, nae doot,' I commented wearily.

'Na, thae E Numbers are bad for yer health; ye've tae avoid them,' he came back.

I was getting desperate for a riposte, staring into my beer at The Elephants' Graveyard, as we called the pub for ageing groovers and '60s relics where we drank at that time. I tried to butt into his flow of half ironic, self-congratulatory rhetoric.

'Aye, but ye've tae admit, there's places I've taen ye as weel . . . broadened yer horizons.'

'Name wan!' he came back categorically.

I searched the beer for inspiration.

'Weel . . . there was Lancet Edge on Aonach Beag . . .'

'A mere romp!' he snorted dismissively. 'Hillwalkers' stuff. It might cause the Munro baggers tae tremble, but not a snow and ice man like mysel'.'

I tried again.

'Weel, I've aye been asking ye tae try the Forcan Ridge . . .'

'The whit?' he inquired. 'Nivver heard o' it!'

'The Forcan Ridge, on the Saddle in Kintail. Under good conditions it's a pleasant winter scramble. Wi' the weather this winter, it should be good. We could ging there next weekend, dae a circuit o' the hale hill . . .'

Davie went silent; he was thinking. After a while, with an air of resignation, he agreed to give it a try.

'The Forcan Ridge,' he mused sadly. 'Did I ever tell ye aboot the time in Crowberry Gully . . .'

The weather held, the frost gripped. Stars in the winter sky brightened the way north to the Fort, where a fish supper was consumed in the car park.

'I didnae bring the Dead Man and the ice screws,' said Davie facetiously, 'I thocht we'd manage withoot them on this trip.'

Along a near-deserted road we went, looking down on Loch Loyne as we crossed to the road to Kintail. There the snow started, fluttering flakes that lay on the frozen road, forcing us to slow down. It was not being driven, but fell as a soft blanket. At Cluanie it was decided to stop for a pint before proceeding to the night's doss.

We took our time, hoping the snow would abate; it got heavier. We waited by the fire, reluctant to step outside into the snow, and got chatting to a couple of lads who were for the Saddle next day as well. They told us they were staying in the Hotel's Bunkhouse, with a bed and cooked breakfast for eight pounds. Beginning to feel the alcohol, fancying more, and opening my jacket to the fire, I rashly said to Davie: 'Fit aboot it, eh? We'll bide here the nicht, and ging tae the bothy the morn, aifter the hill. I fancy a few pints.'

He looked at me as the Ayatollah Khomeini might have looked at Salman Rushdie.

'Stay here? Eight pound? You must be joking. No, we've nivver failed tae get tae oor bothy yet; we'll get there this night.'

Although, as the reader will be aware, Davie is a reasonable man, always open to rational argument, there is the odd occasion when he is immovable. I saw this was that occasion, and guiltily finished my beer.

Whether it was the alcohol, or the darkness after the pub's brightness, but I could have sworn that, outside, Davie hesitated momentarily and looked back to the hotel. But only for a moment, and then he strode boldly on to the car, whose outline was smothered by the falling snow.

We seemed to get ahead of the weather at first. On our way to Kintail, the snow stopped, and the Five Sisters emerged from the night sky to greet us. The steep prow of Faochag stood ahead of us, and next it the Forcan Ridge, which I pointed out to Davie. And again luck was with us as we ascended the Mam Rattagan, negotiating its hairpin bends, which were innocent of snow. We were just in time, however, for as we descended it caught up with us and began to lie in earnest as we turned into Glen More. Luckily a forestry track led to within a mile of our bothy. Along that, past the last habitation, we crawled in the snowfall. When the track stopped, so did we: beside the bridge we were to cross, leading easily to the bothy. Neither of us had been there before, but we would find it easily enough.

Triumphantly Davie emerged from the car, then swiftly slipped back in, his beard rimed like Santa's with snow.

'Ye see, there wis nae need for a hotel. Mind you, it's snowing solidly oot there.'

We changed our clothes in the car, filled the rucksacks and got ready to depart. But before we did, Davie rummaged inside his sack, emerging with the map and compass.

'Let's get going,' I said, stamping the frozen ground with my frozen feet.

'Haud on,' he came back. 'Jist tae be on the safe side, we'll tak' a bearing fae yon brig tae the bothy.'

'But it's nae even a mile!' I protested.

'And it wisnae a mile fae the shelter on Jock's Road that they found the bodies on yon accident in 1950, either,' he came back with, stuffing the compass into his glove.

We crossed the bridge. Stood there, facing the blank screen. Switched on head-torches, so we could at least see each other. Then Davie trudged off in the direction indicated by the compass for a few feet, and I followed. Scrunch, scrunch through the snow went our boots. There was no other sound but occasionally a 'Left', or 'Right', from Davie. Scrunch, scrunch. In these circumstances it is well known that any sense of distance and direction is lost; so too, however, is any sense of time. Scrunch, scrunch. We seemed to have been walking for ages; half an hour perhaps, possibly more? I had forgotten to check the time at the car, to give an idea how long we should take. Just under a mile: twenty minutes, perhaps? Scrunch, scrunch. We must have been going for that already. He stopped, I stopped.

'We could miss that bothy by two feet in this snaw,' I said.

'Aye,' came the response. He looked at his watch. 'We'll gie it anither ten minutes, and then double back on the bearing, hoping we can find yon brig, and doss in the car.'

Scrunch, scrunch. Five minutes. Scrunch, scrunch. A shout from Davie ahead; I approached him.

'A dyke,' he says in triumph.

I am at a loss.

'We cannae sleep ahint a dyke!'

'No, but if there's a dyke, there's a hoose. You follae it wan wye, I'll follae the ither and we're sure tae find the bothy. Keep the torches in sight.'

We headed off, and I soon came to a corner, turned and again followed the stone guide. Turned again at another corner and rashly speeded up, to collide with a wall. The bothy! I located the door, and stood, flashing my head-torch towards its mate blinking like a will o' the wisp through the snow. It bobbed towards me, and we entered the shelter.

'I think,' I said, 'I'd rather hae spent the eight pounds.'

He looked at me as if he had no idea what I was talking about.

Next morning was fine and clear, but windy. Much of the fresh snow had melted lower down, though the hills were white. We decided to drive back round to Kintail rather than start ascending the Saddle from the rear, since to ascend the Forcan Ridge from where we were would involve a complicated cross-country traverse. I passed the time on the return to where we parked, beside the quarry in Glen Shiel, calculating how much of the eight pounds we had each saved had been used up on petrol crossing the Mam Rattagan twice. These deliberations were interrupted, unfinished, by our arrival.

The blue skies scudded with cloud. And the piercing light helped; as did the spindrift curling off the mountain. For the Ridge looked magnificent, foreshortened to seem steeper, and with a backbone of rock stretching the skin of snow.

'A little Aiguilles de Kintail,' mused Davie with approval, as we set off up the stalkers' path, still clear on its lower slopes. Once round the shoulder of Meallan Odhar, the whole sweep of the Saddle Ridge came into view, shattered ridges and gullies choked with snow. Like a woman no longer young, the Scottish hills are better for a little make-up: snow that covers their grassy faults and accentuates their advantages. In both cases we know we are being bewitched, but that nevertheless does not lessen the pleasure of illusion. I was trying to explain this to Davie, but all he came back with was, 'man, ye've got sex on the brain.'

The grandeur of the view hit us, so too did the wind, and we leaned for support on the ice axes we had brought. A lunch break was decided on, and so too was the donning of crampons as a precautionary measure. Davie watched me.

'That's a funny wye ye pit on yer crampon straps. Disnae look secure tae me.'

'It's modern technology Davie, setting up an equilibrium o' forces. Probably nae needed on thae recycled milk crates ye wear.'

For his were not of the newest design, and much repaired. In the mist of such pleasant banter, we noticed two figures descending from the mountain, and watched as they approached us. It was the two lads from Cluanie Hotel, who informed us that the wind on the Ridge was gale force, and they were abandoning their attempt at the Saddle. Davie watched them go.

'That's whit thae hotels dae. Corrode yer will-power. They'll be thinkin o' their lunch and the bath. We've naething tae go back tae, so we maun dae the hill.'

And with this cheery thought we set off, helped for a little by the other lads' footprints.

No one could claim the Forcan Ridge as other than a pleasant romp; but no one could deny either that in winter when under snow and ice it is a dangerous place — and in a wind especially so. The spindrift rapidly became unpleasant, and scarves were wrapped round faces for protection against its sting. Between the gusts the Ridge rose tantalisingly to Sgurr nan Forcan ahead, and we depended heavily on the ice axes for balance against the battering. We got expert at moving as a gust subsided and built up and at leaning against the wedged axe as it reached a crescendo. Conversation was limited to grunts and pointing.

The Ridge rises steeply, then wends its way through the mini aiguilles on a rising col, before sharpening at the summit. But where the Ridge relented, the wind — funnelled — got worse. Out of the shelter of the rocky teeth it was impossible to stand. Desperate remedies were called for, so we got down on our knees. Not to pray, but to get below the wind a little. Heads down, crawling on knees, and using the axe as a third leg, we inched forward to the foot of the summit Ridge, like penitent pilgrims of some obscure religious sect. And our devotions paid off; we reached the last section, where a little shelter enabled us to abandon our undignified and slavish posture, and resume our ascent like men.

'They should bring them here tae train for yon trip tae Lourdes,' was my partner's comment, when we could exchange a word. But there was not much time for talk as we ploughed through the deepening snow to reach the top of the Sgurr nan Forcan.

Before us the ground dropped to a col — thence rising steeply again to the Saddle's summit. The sight was peerless. Out of the swirling mass of spindrift the Saddle would come and go in bright sunshine. And up to the summit, drawing the eye to follow, was a smooth, virgin and horrendously overhanging build up of snow. I thought of expanding on my metaphor of the mountain as a bewitching woman, but desisted. Look we both might with pleasure, but neither of us were prepared to take the chance. We descended to the col, having decided to contour back round to the bealach and return to Glen Shiel.

It was steep, so we faced in, using crampons and axes to descend. On the south side the mountain was windless. I could look down through my legs and see Davie, far below, nearing the bottom. Then suddenly he was going very fast, then suddenly he stopped. I came down as fast as I could, and found him sitting on his doup with a bemused look.

'That's never happened afore,' he muttered, looking at his left crampon, which was hanging loose, having come off on the descent. I allowed myself the luxury of a little chuckle as he repaired the damage to his buckling arrangements. Other damage was repaired by comparing our heroic battle with the retreat of the other party who, Davie had noted with delight, were English.

'Aye, they're no really up tae oor mountains. They underestimate them, especially in winter. Mind you, no that that Ridge is really onything special. Tower Ridge now, in winter, that's different. Have I telt ye aboot the time I did it wi' Al?'

'It's in oor book, Davie, I've read it hunners o' times.'

But he passed the time of the descent down the Coire Mhalagain retelling the story of the epic in winter's darkness; and it was none the worse for a retelling. We got to the car before he got to the Tower Gap.

On the return, we stopped at Cluanie again. The bar was empty, apart from two bored waitresses, whom we chatted to. I must have become animated, for Davie, who had obviously paid more attention to my mountain metaphors than I had thought, commented: 'c'mon now, calm down and let's get going. Remember what ye said about enticing, dangerous bewitchment. We're at the steering clear o' danger stage.'

Back in the car he gave me further advice from the vantage point of his advanced years.

'Steer clear o' waitresses: nothing but trouble. Did I ever tell ye aboot the lassie at Kingshouse, who was a Black MacDonald o' Rannoch? . . .'

I listened. That is the thing about Davie's stories. You can listen to them indefinitely, because they are different every time.

And that is how 'forcan terrible' passed into the restricted vocabulary of the Stobcross Gentlemen's Mountaineering Club.

RATS' FEET ON BROKEN PAST

The trip in was problem enough, but nothing compared to the trip out.

And getting Davie there was harder than getting there.

'There's nae climbing there, and I'm a climber, really. I bet there's some daft Munro there ye havnae done. That's the real reason!'

He had to be persuaded with citations of praise from such as Humble and Murray — men he respected — and by photographs of the sharp, conical hills, before he finally agreed on his first-ever visit to the Glen Affric area.

It was a beautiful spell in late May, the last of the snow retreating from the hills before the new green grass. As we drove north, Davie looked longingly at the familiar landmarks of Glencoe and Nevis, places tried and tested. He was still unsure.

'Whit if we cannae get the bikes?'

'We'll get them.'

From Affric road end to Alltbeithe is a distance of ten miles; to shorten it we had arranged to pick up bikes in Cannich and cycle seven of the miles, cutting time and effort. When we saw the bikes at Cannich, our euphoria, and the need for the roof rack we had carried, vanished. They were kids' bikes, with tiny wheels, and both went in the car with the back seat down. We drove on from Cannich a little chastened.

'I'm glad there's naebody here tae see us,' said Davie when we descended from the car at the Forestry car park at the head of Loch Affric, and he mounted his bike.

'Aye, ye look a bit daft, wi' yer knees abune yer lugs like that,' I replied, to encourage him. It was a fine night, and we breathed in the smell of resin as we set off.

The mechanical advantage — or is it velocity ratio? (school physics are getting a bit rusty) — of the bikes was so small that though they allowed a hair-raising freewheel downhill, and laboriously inched along the flat, dismounting at even the mildest gradient was necessary to push them uphill.

But this gave us time to admire the walk in. The placid loch, edged by sandy beaches. The Caledonian pines, fingering up the hill to grasp at ribbons of waterfall descending from the misty peaks piled up behind Sgurr na Lapaich, and still showing glimpses of snow. Davie was spellbound, and had to admit it.

'I thocht a' these glens were dreich, wi' big roond hills.'

'Nae this ane, it's a jewel.'

We locked the bikes at the ruined shepherd's hut opposite Athnamulloch, and continued on foot, wobbling after the bike run.

'I've arrived at a bothy wi' sair feet afore, but never a sair bum,' Davie complained.

'It's nae really a bothy. It's a Youth Hostel that is only wardened in summer, but left open a' year lang for folk tae use like a bothy, though it's comfier. Ye jist leave a donation.'

I saw Davie wince at the words 'Hostel' and 'donation'.

'Aye, ye've reduced me tae a hillwalker, and noo it's Youth Hostels,' he mused sadly.

I tried another tack. He had recently discovered there was more to Tom Weir than a red nose and woolly pom-pom hat, so I ventured: 'Weir was here in the '30s, fan there was a shepherd and his family in it, wi' a teacher there for the six kids.'

I could see my listener was considering that Humble, Murray and Weir could not all be wrong; and as we walked towards Alltbeithe, his grudging admiration of the scene had quite won him over. The evening sun set behind Beinn Fhada, and honed the peaks of Sgurr a' Bhealaich Dhearg and Ciste Dubh. Davie asked their names. Implicit approval.

'And whit ane is it the morra?' he added wearily, possibly feeling he had been too enthusiastic.

'I thought Sgurr nan Ceathreamhnan and maybe Mullach na Dheiragain if we've time. I havnae done them.'

'I thocht ye'd an ulterior motive for getting me here,' he said triumphantly. 'Munros! It'll be Corbetts next. I actually heard folk in a pub speaking aboot Corbetts,' he added in amazement, as if further comment on moral decay was unnecessary.

It was late when we arrived. We unpacked and went to bed in the warden's room, the only one unoccupied. I awoke to find Davie fussing about the food.

'Fit's up?'

'Some beastie was scuttling amangst the food, I'm wrapping it a' up.'

'Ach, jist cut aff the bits wi' teeth marks, and come back tae bed!'

Despite the cavalier statement we normally took great care with food, protecting it from vermin. This was the one, unacceptable exception. I had the idiotic idea the Hostel would be vermin-free.

Next day dawned cool and clear. We peched our way up the shoulder of Ceathreamhnan, scrunching through the last of the snow, passing the deer moving uphill for summer, and reached the top in a couple of hours. From there the vista from Knoydart to Torridon stretched away; Sgurr na Ciche to the south, Liathach to the north.

'It's big country,' said Davie, impressed.

'Fae Cluanie tae Achnasheen, there's nae through roads.'

We lunched and enjoyed the view. I was dreading the next bit.

'Where to now?' he asked.

I pointed out the outlier, at the end of the ridge leading to Loch Mullardoch. He nearly drapped his peece.

'That's hunners o' miles! Ye're mad!' And then, mildly mollified, 'the things I dae oot o' consideration for my pals. And tae think o' the man I wance was!'

The long and weary ridge to the Mullach cairn was traced, and retraced. Sitting at the loch in Coire nan Dearcag, resting, Davie took a philosophical view.

'Well, at least I'll never hiv tae go there again!'

We rested and watched the deer move across the mountain, before the final ascent and descent, by a stalker's path, to the Hostel.

I felt fine, exercised but not exhausted, invigorated by the clear air. Better when we lit a small fire, for the May evenings are still cold there, and even better when the food we prepared was lying in my stomach. The other occupants of the Hostel returned, chatter started. It had the makings of a good night; we had our drams prepared, and all our stories. Davie could always be relied on to lead the talk in the desired directions, putting all rivals firmly in their places, and ensuring a captive, even captivated, audience. And I had a few special tales. About how I had been there in 1962, when the warden rowed in and out by boat, and dreamed of a donkey to lighten the way.

And how I had returned, 20 years later, to find myself upstaged by a young Italian concert pianist whose father had been there in 1936, after its opening as a Hostel.

Aye, this was what it was all about!

Then, I felt dizzy. So dizzy I excused myself and went to lie down in my bunk. Then I felt sick, and dizzied outside to be sick. Then lay on my bunk again. Then I felt diarrhoea coming and went outside to the chemical toilet, where I stayed a long time. Then I began to sweat, and to shiver and chitter as well. And again the sickness, and again the diarrhoea. All night. And the next day. And all the next night.

I assured Davie I was all right, and encouraged him to make the best of a splendid next day. But I half believed he would use the excuse of ministering to me to avoid more trudging up and down Munros. But off he went, conquering Mam Sodhail and Carn Eighe, finding the deer watcher's hut high on the ridge, and being again impressed.

'Fine big hills, yon.'

Despite my sorry state I could not resist a jibe.

'Aye, ye'll be coontin' next, Davie, tae see foo mony ye've daen.'

He smiled, and for the first time omitted the ritual denial. In the evening I could hear him holding forth ben the hoose, on Forestry privatisation. I could not hear many other voices.

In the morning we had to leave. I was as weak as a baby, and still sweating. Aching in my whole body, and periodically adding my biomass to nature. Three miles seemed like three hundred. The bikes, I thought, it will be fine when we get to the bikes. It will be easy then. It was worse. I could hardly concentrate to stay upright, and the toy bikes weighed a ton when pushed uphill. I had no eyes for the scenery on the way out. Finally the car, and a long drive home, shivering in a blanket and looking frequently for public toilets. Home, and I took to bed for five days, only slowly recovering. I assumed I had had food poisoning.

A couple of months later, Davie read in a newspaper about an estate worker in Sutherland who had died after rat's urine had contaminated his food.

'Listen tae this. Weill's disease, it's ca'd. Shivering, sickness, dizziness and diarrhoea. That's whit ye had.' He quoted: 'In people with weak constitutions, or with heart trouble, failure to receive instant medical attention usually results in death. It was the rat's piss!'

I thought for a minute.
'That's a' richt then.'
'How?'
'My hairt must be fine.'
'Yer no safe on the hills noo. Weill's disease, that Lyme disease fae sheep ticks, Alzheimer's disease fae aluminium in the watter, acid rain . . .'
He carried on in this vein for a while.
'Ye'll no be going back then, tae Alltbeithe?'
'I didnae say that.'
'That's fine, because there's a wee ootlier on a ridge that rins three miles north o' Mam Sodhail that I havnae daen. . . .'

KEEPING CUILLIN DIFFICULTY

There was supposed to be a boat . . .

There was also supposed to be a dozen of us.

The weather eliminated the boat, and winnowed out the dozen.

'Nae commitment,' was Davie's comment. 'If ye say ye're comin, ye come, forbye it's impossible. But Erchie'll arrive, he's a man o' the auld school.'

We were waiting at the Elgol turn-off, watching the squalls from the car, looking at the choppy sea off Broadford, as I enumerated the excuses of about three-quarters of the fellow travellers; excuses that would seem sound good sense to most. But sure enough, there was the Boomerbus drawing up beside us. Erchie too seemed unimpressed by the drop-outs.

'Ach, what's a bit o' weather?'

After giving fifty pence to someone who begged the Postbus fare, and helping a group of the daft English out of a ditch with their car, we three Good Samaritans made our way to the start of the track to Camasunary, and hence Coruisk. I hoped our good deeds would propitiate the gods, and improve the weather; but as we set out it was so bad it was awesome to watch. Huge gouts of cloud were driven before the spiteful wind, throwing down drenching showers; then a metallic brightness of blues and golds would fill the sky, before the next squall. We shoulder-charged the buffeting wind along the path, more like a river along its length, until we looked down on Camasunary.

The sky was filled with dark blueblack clouds. But the coppery shafts of light picked out the dazzling white bothy and ultraverdant grass of the bay. Erchie arrived, and quietly took out his camera. Davie was silent, as if on the proverbial peak in Darien. Ahead, the crown of the Cuillin: how could anything be so black? We descended, past the bothy, and came to the river. Or rather, to where the river should have been. But with the lashing rain, and the incoming tide, a crossing that was whiles a few inches deep was several feet, and of an ever greater width. We walked upstream, to where a few barely-submerged stepping stones led to an islet where the tips of grass were still visible. Donning gaiters and breeches we crossed, largely dry. But not Erchie. Oh, no. He must do the Dance of the Seven Underpants removing breeks and boots, and slithering across in sannies. We watched in amusement, and then left him to re-robe, heading for Coruisk ahead of him.

On rounding the headland, even the cloud, even the squalls turning to steady rain, could not mar the finest view in Britain. The Cuillin horseshoe, holding Scavaig in its grip. It was the first time Davie had been this way, and we scampered over the Bad Step, blethering like wee boys, watching the seals watching us. What did the weather matter? It was Davie's first trip for a couple of years; that in itself was enough for him. We checked, periodically, to see that Erchie was still on the horizon.

Stumbling through the undergrowth and boulders of the next section, we reached the Scavaig River; the rain was by now torrential, and the wind outrageous. If you have come this way, you know the stepping stones at the outlet from Coruisk: a hop, skip and jump. We looked at them now, underwater apart from the huge boulder in the middle of the river breasting the water like a ship's prow. After a silence, Davie spoke.

'In America, we used tae chop doon a tree tae get across.'

'Well, dae ye want tae ging back tae Kilmarie tae get ane?' I suggested.

More silence and thought ensued.

Eventually we decided thus. The upstream side of the stepping stones was thigh deep, but calm; the boulders could be used as a handrail to cross the burn. I donned my helmet. 'In case my heid stotts aff the boulders,' I explained.

We forced our way across the current, and arrived, squelching, at the other side. Davie took the key and headed for the hut: I waited for Erchie. He took a long time coming. It was cold, sitting in the rain. I half dozed, imagined he had fallen off the Bad Step. Woke up. Thought I might have missed him. But there he was, coming slowly towards the river, like an automaton. He sat down on the bank a while, and then, to my amazement, began the Dance of the Seven Underpants again, in the rain. I shouted, 'keep yer beets on, Erchie! It's slippy.'

But he did not hear, or affected not to, and once his dress was in order, began to cross, bent double under his pack, wobbling in the water, threatening to coup at every step. At one point he staggered back and seemed about to fall, but he lurched forwards, grabbed a big boulder, and pulled himself slowly onto it. There he sat, like a gnome on his toadstool, surrounded by the raging, rising waters.

Maybe because he was nearer, or something, Erchie could hear me now.

'Can ye ging back?'

'No.'

'Can ye bide there?'

'A while. It's cauld.'

What to do . . . tell him to shed his pack? Erchie would never do that; it had cost too much, and he never insured. Plunge in the river and pull him out? I doubted my ability, unroped.

'Dinna move, Erchie. I'm gyan for a rope.'

I had this feeling that the stone would be untenanted when I came back; kept seeing it, like a tombstone in the waters, as I ran to the hut.

A cosy scene greeted my eyes. There was Davie with the gas fire on, whisky in hand, regaling a couple of lads with much jollity. The faces, and whisky, dropped when I announced, 'Erchie's stuck in the river. Bring a rope.'

En route back, I realised the newcomers were Kevin, an old Skye pal of mine, and his chum. The latter I recognised as the person who had bounded past us on the way in from Camasunary, leaping from rock to rock. He was all barrel chest and thunder thighs, just the man for a river rescue! So when we reached the bank, and discerned Erchie through the gathering gloom and tempest, he was roped up and sent in to pluck the flower of Coatbridge manhood from the waters. I was getting happier now, no longer alone with the beleaguered.

'Ye've got tae rescue him,' I said, 'he's a category A-listed historical monument.'

Stuart clove the waters with his mighty thighs, and soon reached Erchie. The latter is a bit of a skinnymalink, and not difficult to manoeuvre in water, I imagine. But his rescuer gasped when he donned Erchie's pack, and he buckled under it momentarily.

'What have you got in here, Erchie?' he asked.

He found out later, but for the moment saved his breath for the struggle towards the bank, where they duly arrived. Erchie was shivering and shaking, so we frogmarched him to the hut, where he was changed, fed and sat by the fire, and soon recovered.

I was rummaging in Erchie's pack for his dry clothes, when I found a full, inordinately heavy day pack inside the larger one. I opened it. Inside was a bottle of whisky and myriad cans of beer.

'Erchie,' I gasped, 'I thocht ye left yer dizzen cans o' beer ahint fan the boat didnae materialise?'

'I did. I only took the ten o' them,' came his response. 'And jist the wan whisky bottle.' Then he added, 'I'm glad I kept my bits dry.'

And that is how, for the sake of dry boots and beer, we nearly lost Erchie Boomer.

Next day he was a little fragile, and we left him on a day of dubious weather to do the Dubhs. We had all had our great plans for this trip, but the weather had killed them, and all we hoped for now was an alternation of festering and off-day rambles. It held off as we marched up Loch Coruisk into a monochrome print of grey and black. At the foot of the slabs we stopped, looking up. It promised to be fun. It was, for the first few hundred feet; but after that, it got a bit tedious, especially as we could see nothing in the summit mist. And it was cold, as only a Scottish summer can be. Piercing, damp cold.

'The longest Moderate in the world,' mused Davie on our way down.

'Be positive,' I countered. 'The longest climb in Britain.'

That seemed to cheer him up, but then the rain lashed and lashed at us with its whips, sending us scurrying back to the hut.

When you have got Erchie, Davie and drink, as we had, the evening's entertainment is guaranteed. Davie regaled us with tales of nights on the bare mountain, and of Molly Higgins in Starvation Gulch, while Erchie whetted our appetites with stories of hamster stew in the Andes. And both told Creag Dhu tales, then had disputes about their orthodoxy. Sometimes they had both been there, but one had not noticed the other; sometimes neither had been there, so who is the wiser? We were all listening, helping Erchie lighten his pack for the trip out, a good Christian act, and toasting our feet in J.M.C.S. gas, when there was a knock at the door. I went doorwards, wondering, like the porter in *Macbeth*, who could be abroad on such a night. Then I was faced with two huge black guys, of Harlem Globetrotter physical proportions, dripping in the doorway. I eyed them quickly. Yes, they had baseball boots on. But what were they doing in Coruisk?

They answered my question with one of theirs: 'can we shelter in here for the night?' I recognised Brummie accents. Now, everyone knows J.M.C.S. rules: hanging, drawing and quartering for giving unauthorised access, except in emergency. I decided to see if the rest of the company thought it was an emergency. We were just about to decide that it was, when noises at the door caught our attention. We turned — there were now about a dozen of them! Pushing forward eagerly into the warmth of our Aladdin's cave. As meets secretary, I decided this was too much, and sent them out to pitch camp, adding that if an emergency occurred, they could come back for shelter.

That rather dampened things for a bit. We felt guilty looking out the window at them pitching tents in the hurricane and going to bed without food, while we were as cosy as dormice. But fate took a hand, and eased our consciences. Our two Globetrotters, either less competent or smarter than the rest, collapsed their tent trying to erect it, and soon appeared again asking for mercy, which we bestowed; bestowed with ministrations of food, libations of whisky and benedictions of travellers' tales. Struggling with the accents and with the unlikely events, the lads looked as though they thought they had landed on the moon, or in a madhouse. But they kept these thoughts to themselves, and themselves near to the fire. We discovered it was their first trip — ever — to Scottish hills.

In the morning they were to set off back to Sligachan, but first disappeared into their sodden encampment. Then returned with a request and a present. Firstly, they asked for all our autographs, to show their mother, for saving their lives as they put it. We awkwardly obliged. Then they presented us with a couple of full bottles of . . . mineral water, for our use. We were speechless. Outside were billion upon billion of gallons of the stuff, and they had carried this all the way from Sligachan in their baseball boots.

'Thanks,' I think somebody managed to say, before they departed with their autographs and memories.

A little later, Davie said to Erchie, 'is that no jist the daftest thing ye've ever seen. Carrying a' that unnecessary liquid and extra weight in tae Coruisk?'

'Aye,' agreed Erchie opening a preprandial can of lager. 'Some folk hiv nae sense.'

The rest of that day we watched mesmeric rain; sheets, blankets of it, cascading round the mountains. Discussed how much further the Mad Burn had risen since the last time we looked. Dozed, washed, read the old J.M.C.S. mags. In a word, had a good fester. And felt the better of it.

'Nae weans, nae work,' Davie summed it up.

He was taking the bad weather more philosophically than I had anticipated.

But next day, to our surprise, the cloud had risen, though it was still a leaden dull day, with a smirr of rain. Davie surprised me once again when he said, 'Come on, get yer bits on. We'll get yer Pinnacle done, if naething else this trip.'

Unable to think of a credible excuse, I prepared with the rest of them. Kevin and Stuart went off back to Glen Brittle, Erchie came with us as far as the Dubhs and headed off for a solo scramble. Davie and I continued to the head of Loch Coruisk, ringed by black towers, and moved up into the primeval wilderness of Coireachan Ruadha. It looked a setting worthy of Tyrannosaurus Rex, and I would not have been surprised by pterodactyls flying overhead.

We stumbled over the boulders and stopped to look at the Coireachan Ruadha face, covered with a fine film of moving water, and listened to the symphony of the drips and drops from the crags. Davie's eyes had a particular look in them.

'I dinna suppose I'll ever get Fluted Buttress done now. If ye get the right conditions, it's the wrang partner; the wrang conditions the right partner. Never seems tae work oot.'

I charitably interpreted today as one with the wrong conditions, rather than the wrong partner, though I knew it was both. I had my own worries. There were miles of scree ahead, before the Bealach Coire na Banachdich gully. It was drizzling, it was cold. I was miserable. But Davie seemed to entertain no doubts as we ploughed on, meeting, seeing, not a soul. Till heading for Sgurr Dearg from the col we met a man with a stick and dark glasses, who asked us the way to Glen Brittle. . . .

At the foot of the Pinnacle, I sat and started to make myself comfortable for lunch, while I waited for my partner. It had taken us four hours to get to this point. The wind was now rising, the mist obscured all but the first few feet of the monolith. We would come back another day, I thought, as I munched my sandwich.

Davie arrived. Dumped his sack. Started uncoiling the rope, picked out a couple of slings, unceremoniously ordered me off my butt end.

'But Davie, it's cauld, it'll be miserable.'

'D'ye want tae dae it?'
'And it's weet and windy as weel!'
'D'ye want tae dae it?'
'It's nae the getting up. Ye ken I'm a' richt tae mild severe, wi' a' my infirmities and inadequacies. It's the gettin doon. I'm no happy wi' the abseiling, especially on a day like this.'
'I didnae ask for a speech, but if ye wanted tae dae it. I've walked four hours here, it'll be as lang back. I'm no coming here wi' ye again.'

And he headed downhill towards the foot of the petrified dinosaur we were to climb.

I stood frozen, after tying on to the rope end he had left behind, then followed. It was greasy, the wind gave sharp nudges in the ribs; and now the bloody rain came on again! I was spared exposure; on each side I could see about six feet to where the mist swirled over the void. And I slipped and slithered to the top, where Davie sat belayed to the detached block. I expected a rest, deserved one I thought.

'Richt, get doon,' ordered my first man, fixing me into a sit sling and pointing towards a cauldron of mist and adding, 'I'm frozen waiting for ye.'

Without thinking I moved down the sloping ramp; that was easy, and I could still see Davie's surly, reassuring face. Then at the perpendicular, or rather incut edge, I stopped to think, had a wee look below. Did not like what I saw, and asked politely if I could come back up?

Davie swore all the curses known to man, and added a few of his own recent invention, ending with: 'Get the —— doon there, and dinna come back!'

So, as any man would between a rappel and Davie's wrath, I chose the descent into the void, pushed off edgily. Slid down the rope, pushed again, speeded up. Hey, this was a dawdle! And great fun! A little push again and . . . help! I'm birling round and round on the rope, now seeing the pinnacle, now seeing nothing but mist. Slither, slither, push, thump. I am on the ground. Quite fancy doing it again, but hesitate to ask Davie to wait for me to come back up. Unrope and lie there a while. Do not need to come back to Skye again, done all my Cuillin Munros. But I will, hundreds of times. Even if I have to come in a bogey.

Davie appears. I had forgotten about Davie.
'Thanks for the rope.'
'Sorry for shouting at ye.'

He has never apologised to me before, yet he never had less need to.

We toil back to the hut under a lifting sky. It looks set fair for tomorrow. At Coruisk, there is a boat moored in the loch. A piper is walking round the decks, playing, and the music reverberates off the gabbro slabs of the hills. After a meal, I try unsuccessfully to fish, and have a chat with the piper. It keeps the midgies away, he says. On the shore is a party dossing down for an attempt at the Ridge next day. They'll be in luck weatherwise.

And they are: a day of unparalleled magnificence greets our plans for departure. Azure skies and a light breeze, the mono-chrome become technicolour around us. The river is down, the Boomer Stone accessible now dry shod. We take our time going out, to enjoy the day. Cross again at Camasunary with water below the welts of our boots. At the bothy we meet an occupant and get invited in for a cup of tea. Quickly we realise these are not our fellow mountaineers, but a group becoming increasingly common in bothies, bred of the Thatcher years. Guys out of work, living in bothies, collecting (as these were) buckies for fishmongers, or doing odd jobs. Even begging, as one told us unashamedly. 'It's not as if I'm a mass murderer, is it?'

We recognise him as the beggar of fifty pence for the Postbus. And one of them tells us he is building a log cabin in the wilderness, in central Scotland, and it is almost finished. A new generation of hobos and tramps, just as the one of the 1930s withers away. They put our weekend hoboing, underpinned by work, mortgages and good gear, into relief.

Back at the cars, I suggested: 'a few wee incidents tae remember in yon trip.'

'True,' came back Davie. 'Them as didnae come is the losers.'

'Aye,' Erchie summed it up, 'what's a bit o' weather? As lang as ye get on the hill?'

And the next time, there might well be a boat.

CROSSING THE RIVER

The weather was not good. High winds were forecast to become gales, driving the lashing rain before them. Ten people had been killed in avalanches the previous weekend. But we wanted to get away, to get on the hill again.

'Let's jist mak' it an overnight at the 'Ville,' I suggested. 'We havnae been there for ages, and we can visit the Kingie on the wye up, and Inverarnan on the wye doon, see if there's onybody for pints and crack . . .'

Davie was unsure. In his demonology an 'overnighter' was just slightly less depraved than a 'day-outer'; only a 'weekender' could claim to be a real mountain man. But the horrendous Friday weather, and worse forecast for Saturday, led us to travel north on the Saturday night, hoping that it would ease for the Sunday.

For once, we had made the right decision. As we drove north through the torrential rain, the hills were invisible. At the Rannoch Moor, the wind appeared to wish to pick up the car and throw it into the barren wastes beside the road, as if resenting our intrusion. Entering the pub in the Kingshouse got us drenched. We shivered awhile in that bar which has all the charm of a public toilet, and is as cold, and began to think of leaving.

'Yon river will be high,' said Davie. 'I dinnae want tae cross it fou.'

A couple of young lads were discussing a route. They were so wide shouldered and narrow waisted, they looked triangular.

'I was quite disappointed,' one said, 'it was only E3 or 4.'

'Time for us tae leave,' remarked Davie, drinking up.

But fate took a hand. In came Conn Higgins, an old mate of Davie from way back, just home from America to look after his ill mammie, and picking up the traces after ten years away from Glencoe. Pints were ordered, crowds gathered round our celebrity.

'Did Crowberry last week, Davie. First time. Never did it when it was popular, couldnae stand the crowds. Might go to the Ben the morra for Zero . . .'

The river was still rising with the rain. But the pints were going down, the barman was giving large measures of whisky, and the pub seemed to be getting warmer and cosier. Between drinks, Davie muttered ritual incantations about going.

'Crossing the river, are ye?' asked Conn.

'Ye've got tae cross the river,' Davie uttered a little tipsily, with as much sang-froid as he could summon. 'We should be getting going.'

But at that point in came Benny, dazzling in that season's Goretex jacket, a coat of many colours. The message we had left on his yuppie answering machine had got him into his yuppie GT-whatever, and got him there. More introductions, more pints reluctantly agreed to. Then someone started a rumour the pub was closing, but there was a disco in the lounge. Alright, we would go through for one more drink, before heading for the river and the 'Ville, alright . . .

It was warm in the lounge. Benny and Conn, single men, were the first to notice that there were women there; some teachers' walking club's annual dinner. Some were dancing with other women, therefore . . . One could almost read their thoughts. Davie was swithering after four pints and three whiskies, and I overheard him trying to convince Conn to cross the river.

'Naw, I'll stay here and hae a few mair. Get a kip someway, under the kitchen table or something.'

'But Conn, it's tradition. Ye've tae keep using the 'Ville, keep crossing the river . . .'

'Naw, naething sacred aboot that place. Too many ghosts anyway.'

He tried Benny.

'C'mon, Benny, the river's high, come wi' men that can cross it blindfold.'

'I'll jist have anither pint and then come, dinnae wait for me,' came from Benny, distracted, his eyes on the dance floor.

We left alone.

'Sex,' muttered Davie, disgusted, wobbling a little. 'And they'll get naewye wi' that lot. Didnae fancy ony o' them anyway. That river, that's the important thing. . . . If ye canne dae that, ye're finished!'

I was driving, and sober. We came to the lay-by where the path led down to the Jacksonville river. I was sober, I could see the rain pelting down, could hear the roar of the river: see the silver band of its height in the middle distance. I was sober. Changing Davie's mind requires all the skills of a practised diplomat; if ever I manage, I will apply for the Diplomatic Corps.

'Davie,' I suggested, gently, 'the watter's afa high. Listen tae it.'

I stopped for effect. We listened to the roar.

'We've got tae cross, we've nae alternative.'

Was this a weakening?

'We could drive tae the Brig o' Orchy, and kip doon in the station waiting room . . .'

My trump card. But my partner was unimpressed.

'We've said, in public, we were gyan tae cross the river . . .'

'We can tell a lee . . .'

'Naw, for that ye need imagination. I'll gae doon and check it first, and see.'

He disappeared, and I half expected never to see him again. What if he fell in and was swept away? I should have gone with him, but was glad, as I sat watching the Buachaille frowning through the mirk, that I had not. It was sleeting now, and the car was rocking with the wind.

He reappeared, and even through the sleet I could see he was happy, smiling. That was bad news.

'C'mon, it's naething. Get ready and let's go.'

I stripped to my underpants; my heart was as low as the jeans at my feet. I donned my wellingtons, rolled right down to prevent them filling with water. Lifted my pack. I was cold, shivering. I thought of Benny and Conn: the warmth, the lights, the women — even though I had not fancied them much either. But Davie was off and I must needs do likewise since he knew the arcane route across the river, following the gravel bank downstream in shallower water. I took a walking stick for balance, and headed off after him.

He stood at the bank, light from headtorch on the water showing nothing but slanting sleet. My torch showed nothing either, except the speed of the flow.

'This is the highest I've seen it,' he said, 'but it'll still be a' right. Gie's yer airm.'

We linked arms and gripped each other's shoulders, stepped in. It was melt water, from February snow. I wanted to scream with the pain of it, as we sidled down the gravel bank, the water knee high, moving slowly, a step at a time. The bank ended, and thence it was a direct line to the shore. Now it deepened, and the flow was swifter. I leaned against the walking stick and we descended into deeper water. A pair of ice tongs caught my balls and gripped them; it was like being burned, and this time I did cry out in pain, stumbled forward. Grasped the tussocky divots of the bank where it had collapsed into the river. Pulled myself out and sat awhile.

'That was nae bother, eh?' chirped Davie cheerily.

I heard someone agreeing with him.

The 'Ville was a slum. Windows broken, lath ripped out for firewood, pools of water on the floor. When I got in Davie was dancing a jig or Highland fling in the middle of the doss — out of delight, or the desire to get circulation going, I was too miserable to ask. He seemed to have become tipsy again, after an interlude of sobriety.

'We did it, we did it! And Higgins didnae, and there's nae sign o' Benny. We did it! This is whit it's a' aboot, nae sex. It's aboot crossing the river. This is whit shows yer still alive and kickin.'

He carried on in this vein for some time, while I rolled out my sleeping bag on a dry corner of the floor, crawled in and tried to regain my body heat. I heard voices in the night making a concerto with the symphonic background of the river, but no one came. Maybe I was dreaming. Dave slept deep and long, and snored, untroubled.

Grubby rays of sun fingered in the broken window as I opened unwilling eyes. A huge cocoon lay in the middle of the wet floor. I poked it. No butterfly, but Benny emerged from its feathered depths. This was his tale.

He had entrapped, he thought, a maturish woman and was thinking about bites-of-cherry and velvet-off-antlers, giving it laldy on the dance floor and a wee cuddle forbye, when up steps her husband, threatening fisticuffs and demanding he desist. He did; and, disappointed in love, headed for the lay-by where he had left his car. Much the worse for drink, he staggered down to the river; the voices I heard were his calls across to us. Receiving no answer, he plunged directly into the river. He is a wee fella, Benny, and he was soon oxter-high and heading downstream at a great rate. Luckily he was swept to the bank. He decided to give the crossing a miss, and head upstream to Lagangarbh, crossing by the bridge at the S.M.C. hut. Only a mile upstream and a mile back down, he thought.

He plunged into peat hags in the dark, fell into raging side burns, staggered across rutted heather. A change of plan: he would fight back up to the road, leave his pack, go back for his car, drive up to Lagangarbh. So, he dumped the pack at the roadside and jogged, in his underpants, back to his car. Then he could not find the pack in the dark. He eventually reversed over it with the car. The other side of the river, when he got there, was worse, with the melt coming off the Buachaille. He fell several times before getting to the hut at 4.30 in the morning. Four hours to come a hundred yards. Davie was delighted.

'Ye should hae come wi' us. Women are naething but trouble. Aye, Benny, ye can run up the VS's, but ye cannae cross the Jacksonville River. Ye're illegitimate, ye're nae baptised.'

I looked at the rafters. There, on a hook, hung a pair of underpants that had dripped a large pool on the floor. They were black, and looked as if a pair of boots had been cleaned with them.

'That lassie didnae know what she was missing,' I observed.

He had made it, but he was more knackered than from any night of love. Benny decided that a nice breakfast in the Fort, followed by a sauna and a trip to the climbing wall, was to be his day's effort. It sounded a great idea to me. The weather had improved a little. The wind had dropped, and squalls replaced the constant rain, but it was still unpleasant. You used to be able to rely on Davie on such days, but something has got into him of late, and he will not hear of a climb-down.

'We'll hae a go at yon Stob Bhan in the Mamores, I've aye fancied the look o' it. A sauna is nae training for crossing the river. And I bet Higgins is lying drunk under some table. He'll no be on the hill the day.'

But he was. While Benny was in the sauna, Conn was on Orion Face. And was blown off on the descent, cracking his pelvis.

Davie was right. Stob Bahn is a fine-looking hill. However, we could not see it as we left the car at Polldubh, in the sleet and the wind. The weather was so awful, I was quite cheery. I could not see Davie continuing more than a short while. We squelched and slithered up the path, and then Davie saw a rainbow.

'Look,' he said, 'that's a good sign!'

'No it's nae,' I replied. 'It means fire next time, and that we've got aff lightly sae far.'

But by the time we reached the sugary snow the mist had lifted, and we could see the expanses of snow sloping up to the col, curled back with a cornice. The rocky defiles of the three sharp prows of the mountain were even beginning to appear, though not the summit.

'Ye see,' said Davie, 'if ye cross the river and fight the good fight, ye get rewarded.'

'It's nae a mechanistic, moral universe, Davie. Rewarding good and punishing evil.'

'It is! It is!' he insisted, as we plodded up the stalkers' path to the snowfield below the col.

This was not steep, and the snow gave good grip; but a couple of lads without axes who had followed us hesitated and returned. We kicked steps up to below the cornice, which was cracked, and traversed below it till we gained safe access to the ridge. Here all hell broke loose. The wind raged wildly, and the sleet thickened the mist to impenetrability. Now and again the steep prow of Stob Ban reared out of the mist, looking quite Alpine in the distorting mirror of the weather. We were walking along in silence, heads down to the wind, when I saw Davie stop and point with his axe.

'Oops,' he said.

He was indicating a huge crack, a virtual crevasse, on our left. On our right, what we thought was a safe ten feet away, was the edge of the cornice. We were on it, between edge and crack. Gingerly we moved inwards.

Now only the prow lay ahead, and we crunched up through boulder and snow. A short gully slanted leftwards the final few feet to the summit plateau, and we made for it, when the wind got up again. But this time it did not bring sleet or snow, but an uplift that broke and then scattered the mist. I saw Davie's big bucket steps ahead of me, ploughing through brilliant white snow below a soft blue sky. When I joined him at the summit, he observed, 'ye see, it is a moral universe.'

It certainly was a stunning one. Southwards the Aonach Eagach Ridge sliced the sky in two, while to the north the ridges of the Ben peeped over its massy bulk. Loch Eil silvered away to the west, though it was still unclear eastwards whence the weather was coming. We started back as soon as our little window of visibility was closed. We scampered down, and glissaded much of the descent to below the snow. Here it began to rain, foul, driven rain. At the car, heaps of sodden gear lay on the muddy ground, steaming, as we changed into dry clothes.

'Benny missed himself, eh?' suggested Davie.

I do not, however, think Benny would have seen it that way somehow.

We warmed up at the fire at Inverarnan with food and drink, before heading home. We had crossed the river. The universe was a moral one, at least now and again.

CROWBERRY CURFEW

I had always fancied it. Fancied it for that one move. Ever since seeing the famous photograph of the bauldy fella belaying his partner who is disappearing round the corner off Abraham's Ledge. It was everything, as I read the Gude Book, that I was hopeless at: a leftward, committing move round a blind corner, and then an upward move towards unseen holds. So I knew that if I could get there, I would experience the full integrity of my emotions: fear.

He was a bit unenthusiastic. Not about the climb — he had done it before of course. But he was busy with the flitting, and was not sure if he could fit a day in. And then the weather forecast was bad for the Monday we had planned, as he told me on the phone on the Sunday night.

But the Monday was fine, my enthusiasm triumphing over Met. gloom. I waited for him to descend to the car. He came down, and loaded up the car: then came back down and placed the apple of his eye in the baby seat, saying, as we headed off to the child minder, 'life's no as straightforward as it used tae be.'

So with one thing and another it was midday before we even got to Glencoe, wading the river to the Ville, with the pebbles hardly covering the stream's flow. It promised well; the cloud was high, and the sun came and went. A cool breeze fanned us. The huge mass of the Buachaille rose before us, inviting and dry as a bone. No excuses today, I thought, as we passed the Ville, where an attempt had been made to repair some of the ravages of winter and vandalism. But we hurried on; we were late starting.

The moor was crisp and soon we crossed the Waterslide Slab, virtually bone dry underfoot. Davie led us round and then past the foot of Curved Ridge, where we met the only other party of the day. She was following him up the Ridge, an enormous rope's length of a run out behind him. She did not look too happy.

'Just take it Alpine style, carry the rope with you,' her partner encouraged.

Whether he was distracted by watching them, or just had other things on his mind, Davie took us a little too high on the maze of paths between Curved Ridge and Crowberry, and we had to climb down a little to the foot of the latter. Here we sat to lunch. Opposite, great orange bats were coming down from high behind Altnafeidh, and landing beside the Ville.

'Hang gliders,' said Davie. 'Imagine daeing yon, when you could be up here.'

We happed up for the climb, and he donned his helmet.

'A Daddy's headwear,' he smiled. 'Nae mair eight-piece bunnets wi' a folded *Daily Record* inside. That's whit we used tae use in the Dolomites for stonefall.'

Then he set off up the first pitch, a steep wall, but with big jugs all the way. Despite a long lay-off, he moved up quite quickly, though I noted he was putting in more protection than he might have formerly. That is the job of the second man that I hate: tottering on some wee ledge trying to extricate one of Davie's belays. They were good — most of them would hold the QE2 — so they are a scunner to get out.

But after a short run out, I heard him cry delightedly, 'the Ledge of the Gods! The Ledge of the Gods! Get yersel up here quick man, in the steps of the pioneers.'

So I scampered up, and soon was beside him in that peerless situation. A rock ledge hanging over a near vertical drop, with seemingly no means of escape. Above was an apparently holdless wall, while the ledge itself — about five feet long and maybe a couple at the most wide — petered out at the far end of the wall. There was hardly room for us both and our gear. Where on earth had the the Reverend Robertson, who took the famous picture, perched himself and his tripod, I wondered?

But there was no time to muse on photographic history — Davie was moving along the ledge. I noticed a few sloping footholds on the slab where the wall ended, but there was not much for hands, I remarked.

'I wish I could get a runner in,' Davie said.

'Och, ye'll dance roon. Ye've done it afore,' I encouraged, with the optimism of the safe, second man. I was always desperate for him to get round the crux quick, when we arrived at it on a climb.

'Aye, but I wisnae leading it,' he confessed, stepping back to the ledge.

'Oh,' I thought, checked my belay and paid a little more

attention to the rope than was my wont. It is not true, as Davie claims, that he once looked down and saw me belaying him with my hands in my pockets, but sometimes my attention does wander.

'It's the confidence I hae in ye,' I would counter. 'I ken ye'll nae fa'.'

When I looked up from my belay, he was gone, vanished. My heart thumped in my chest as the rope played out, slowly, then stopped. He was obviously at the move-up, not a place to linger on poor holds. Then relief flowed as the rope did for a while, then stopped again. He was there. My invariable feeling when Davie has done a crux, is then to wish he had not — since I now have to follow. What if there is no stance round that corner? There must be, he has done it! What if there are no pull-up holds afterwards, or they are too high? He is smaller than me, so I must be able to reach them! Christ, there isn't much for the hands, and these stances slope a bit. What a drop! Don't look down, look up. There's nothing there, it's smooth and holdless.

'Davie, far's the hauds?' I shout rather stupidly.

'Jist move up, they'll appear.'

My legs were beginning to wobble, so on faith and a prayer I did so. And there they were, gorgeous big holds that enabled me to pull myself up beside my partner, who clipped me onto the belay as I probably betrayed more of my fear than was manly to do. But we are post-macho men, I thought. We can be more honest with our emotions than the sturdy pioneers.

'That's aboot it, the rest is a scramble,' he reassured, ministering to the rope and the rest of the gear.

And that was about it. We took it slowly, moving up the good rock to the foot of Crowberry Tower, and then scampering delightedly up to that easy but dramatic stance for a snack and snaps. I thought now might be the time.

'Let's go to the summit Davie,' I suggested.

'Naw, naw. Ye've been reading too much o' thae auld S.M.C. articles, wi' doughty pioneers aye visiting the summit. Naw, I'm in a hurry tae be doon. We'll gae doon Curved Ridge.'

I hate Curved Ridge. Not going up, that is a fine easy scramble, with First Circle seats to watch the climbers on Rannoch Wall. But coming down is different. It is steep in parts, and those parts are polished to the consistency of verglas in my opinion. Easy, but one wee slip and the penalty clause is unthinkable. If we went to the summit, I could then argue for a descent by Lagangarbh Corrie — just a walk.

So that started it. I was miffed, and a bit put out by the 'early home' reference; wasn't this supposed to be a day out? Davie shot off down Curved Ridge, as if trying to beat the record for a descent. I cautiously followed, inching my way on the polished rock, and swearing never to come down this way again. It had been a fine day, but now the few clouds were peeled off the sky, and the sun began to beat down fiercely. I was still fully harnessed and helmeted, and was getting sweaty. Besides, that bugger Davie had left me with the rope as usual. Where was he? Christ, he's miles ahead, I thought, stumbling about at the foot of Curved Ridge where I had finally arrived. Why does the bugger not wait for me? I am faster up the hill, he faster down. But I always wait for him, I thought, self-righteously.

He had waited for me by the Ville. I arrived, dripping sweat and in a foul temper.

'Let's ging doon tae the Coupal brig for a dook,' I suggested. I was longing for a swim.

'Naw, naw, let's nae bother. Let's jist get haim.'

'Why nae?' — I confess I snapped it out.

'Ye cannae hae everything in wan day. Ye've sat in the sun on tap o' Crowberry Tower, that should satisfy ye.'

It was his car, so I could not argue. But I sulked silently across the Rannoch Moor. Davie said nothing either.

At Crianlarich I said, 'I want tae stop for a pint at Inverarnan.'

'A' right,' said Davie, looking at his watch — it was 5.30 — 'but jist wan.'

We stopped and I bought the driver a pint, and one for myself, ordering food as well. I was beginning to feel a bit silly, but I was locked in my sulk, unable to stop, like picking scabs. As I finished, Davie checked his watch again. But he had been bought a drink, and honour forced him to say, 'dae ye want anither wan?'

Honour should have made me refuse. It did not.

'Yes.'

I watched him at the bar. I was behaving abominably. He had, when he was fashed with other things, driven me there and led me up something I could never have hoped to do on my own. And here was I sulking for lack of a swim. 'You bastard, you bastard,' I said of myself to myself as he brought me Guinness.

I downed it in two great swigs.

'Let's go,' I said.

We chatted as we drove back down the road, doing 80 on the straight stretches, both hoping he would beat the curfew.

A SHORT WALK WITH OUR PUBLISHER

We were headed for the Fort, to do a 'signing' of our new book. I could detect a certain disquiet in Davie.

'We're gettin awfae respectable,' he suddenly said, pausing to gather his thoughts and measure his words. 'Signings, nominated for literary prizes, folk writing aboot us in the S.M.C. Journal, and now . . .' — he stopped — 'now gawn tae the C.I.C. hut wi' a member o' that very organisation. We'll be losing oor bothy-credibility, folk will think we've selt oot.'

So that was what was worrying him.

'Nonsense, Davie,' I replied. 'Ye've jist got tae learn tae handle fame — the signings, the literary luncheons, the interviews . . . and we can keep a fit in baith camps: ging tae a bothy noo and again, jist tae show we've nae lost the common touch.'

'And this signing. Folk we've upset in the first book could turn up and attack us.'

'I widnae think so, and if they did, it wid be guid publicity. Mair like we'll be sittin there, twiddlin' oor thoombs.'

Arrival at the Gold Mine in the main street of the Fort, with its equipment shop, restaurant and bar, ended the agonised discussion. We introduced ourselves, and repaired to the restaurant for a quick lunch. Davie chose with care and parsimony.

'Times are hard oot at Spam Valley,' he quipped.

But at the till, the waitress waved us past, announcing that the manageress had told her it was free for the authors. Davie was downcast.

'If I'd known that, I'd have taen mair. D'ye think I could gae back?'

'That micht nae look guid, Davie. But here ye are, yer first introduction tae the gravy train: a free bap and plate o' soup in the Fort. And this is jist the beginning.'

But we had chosen the quietest afternoon of the summer: it was a glorious day, late in the season, the holidays were over. We sat beside our display of books, while a trickle of customers passed, and a handful bought. Davie browsed the shelves, pretending he was not with me. Inured by a youth paper-selling outside factory gates, I did not mind it so much. But Davie was downcast.

'Middle-aged wummen is a' we're gettin'. We're no attracting the glamour factor' — and he pointed out a group of lip-glossed young lovelies investigating the natural beauty products, oblivious to our magnetic attractions. I sent him off to get the football results, and manned the fort alone.

Our publishers arrived, we called it a day, and decided to eat in the Gold Mine before heading for the hut. Davie piled his tray with grub as a consolation for the poor sales; but was doubly downcast when a new waitress charged him the full whack, obviously not having been instructed to feed us free again. We ate in silence for a while, until our publisher announced: 'there's eight members of the Pinnacle Club in the hut tonight.'

Now our publisher is a man you could trust your wife, daughter and life savings with. A man with the mein and integrity — though not the social attitudes — of an Eton headmaster: a man whose word you could take. An earnest man. Davie began to cheer up, for the Pinnacles are a famous climbing club of a female sexual persuasion.

'Two each,' he said quietly, then added, 'we'd better get started, it'll be dark by nine.'

Now the problem arose. Our publisher and his partner had decided to reach the hut by the tourist path from Glen Nevis, rounding Meal an t-Suidhe, and then descending to the hut: this was shorter, and the path better. I decided to go to the toilet while Davie argued against this, for I knew what he would say anyway. That this meant gaining and losing height, that it meant putting foot on the dreaded TOURIST path, that it wasn't traditional, that you didn't get any views that way. I returned, asked, 'fit wye is it, Davie?'

'The wye we aye go!'

So we split from our publishers, with Davie pointing out that it was not a race, and that he was very unfit, and doubted even if he would make the C.I.C. hut at all. We would see them there.

'Get the tea on for us,' was Davie's parting shot.

We got stuck in a traffic jam outside the Fort. Davie was fuming, cursing. When I pointed out there was no hurry, he fixed me with a steely stare.

'It's nae race, but I still want tae be first there!'

And first we were, by a long shot. It took us two hours, fifty per cent off my previous best time to the hut. We were helped by light packs, by the freshness of the evening, and, I suspect also, by the promise of the Pinnacles.

It was a fine evening as we passed through the Distillery, the Angel's Dram filling the air with the scent of the brewst. As we crossed the railway into the Everglades, the tang of the bog myrtle then filled our nostrils. Ahead we could see the ridges of the Ben, dark under a heavy sky, pressed down under the mist, black as hell and as dramatic.

'Ye dinnae see this fae yon daft tourist path,' Davie spat out in disgust, as we passed the high dam and began ascending the Allt a' Mhuilin, slowly feeling the hill envelop us in its dark embrace. Huge, threatening pinnacles towered over us as we entered the hut.

But there were none inside it. Only four members of the Ferranti Climbing Club. Davie glowered at them as if they were to blame.

'We were expecting eight wummen here,' he said, accusingly, looking around — possibly expecting they were hidden somewhere. There was a silence as the Ferranti lads looked at one another, then:

'Sorry,' one said, rather apologetically.

'Ach, nivver mind,' Davie said, excusing them their shortcomings. 'I'm getting used tae disappointments.'

'Here,' I comforted him, 'hae a wee snifter and that'll cheer ye up.'

I pulled out the bottle of Macallan that constituted the bulk of my supplies for the 'overnight' and passed him a dram. After his usual complaints about the price of the whisky I bought, he paid compliment to its quality by removing it from the bottle at a great rate. We were well down it when our publishers entered, to be greeted by demands for clarification on the Pinnacle question; they assured us they had been given the information in good faith by the hut custodian. But was that the ghost of a smile I saw playing round the lips of the Eton schoolmaster's face? It did not stay there long, for it was followed by a slight loss of sang-froid when the Macallan was noticed, and from the depths of his own pack was produced — a miniature of Glenfiddich. I allowed myself the luxury of a little revenge banter.

'Jist look at that, Davie, the official S.M.C. cairry-oot' — pointing to the Publisher's Dram.

'Aye, but they're auld men, they've tae save their strength for the morra,' replied Davie, indulgently.

Disappointment at the presence of the ballistic missile men gradually faded, and Davie, for their edification — since they were from Auld Reekie — gave them the unofficial history of every offside goal scored against the Hearts in the last thirty years. This was followed by some unpublished tales of nights on the bare mountain, of Matterhorn north face descents, of river crossings in Canada sharing log rafts with bears, and other tales I will get him to write down some day. Our publisher was politely listening, prodding, thinking that there might be another book for him in all this. While publishers and missile men prepared to bed down, Davie and I performed the good Christian act of finishing for the Ferranti team a half bottle of Bowmore that their combined efforts appeared incapable of exhausting. A dodgy mantelshelf move from the table to the bunk, and then it was lights out.

In the morning, problems: one publisher very unwell, with all the symptoms of altitude sickness — at 2,000 feet. The other teamed up with Davie and me, but the mist and drizzle was right down to the hut, the cliffs clagged in, the rock running with wet. We waited a little while over a lingering breakfast, and then headed up into Coire Leis, hoping it would clear for a scramble up North-east Buttress, which Davie had never done.

'There's things a man has gotta do,' he announced, 'and the Man Trap is wan o' them.'

I headed off in advance into the mist, and soon lost sight of my companions as I scrambled up the scree slopes, looking for the abseil posts leading to Carn Mor Dearg arete. Occasionally there were fragments of visibility, and below I could hear voices. Or rather, Davie's voice — and little snatches of names and places that let me know our publisher was being regaled with stories even at this early hour. And was it the mist baffling the voices, or did I really hear, 'you should get all this down, Davie . . .'?

It was not going to clear: we reached the arete without seeing a single abseil post. The rock was slippy, even to stand on. North-east Buttress was out of the question. But to stretch the legs there was the arete to Carn Mor Dearg, and then down to the hut.

'It's a fine wee scramble, Davie, and on a clear day ye can see Muriel Gray fae the tap. It gie'd her a fricht, so if ye ever meet, ye'll be able tae haud yer heid up high.'

I knew mention of the lady in question would get Davie in a lather, so I moved along the arete, leaving him to explain to our publisher where Murielphobia fitted in to Davie's peculiar *Weltanschauung*. No connection between Hearts' offside goals and Muriel's Munros? Give Davie half an hour and you'll eat your words.

The arete was greasy with moisture, and needed care at points: you could see, as our publisher claimed, that it could be tricky in winter. Indeed a friend of his was killed falling from it when a crampon fouled in a gaiter, and sent him headlong. It was better for the mist, which made the arete seem less broken and acutely angled than it was. We scrambled along, then suddenly a wind scooped all the mist out of the bowl between our mountain and the Aonachs, leaving the arete as the dividing line between clear skies and blanket mist, rising like a prow to the summit. It was a moment of magic, but gone before the camera could record it. Brief thoughts that we had erred, and that the day would clear, were smothered as the mist fell again. At the top, Davie passed judgement.

'It maintained its interest a' the wye. And tae think o' a' the years I've been comin up here, and nae done it.'

'Ye see Muriel in a new licht noo, eh Davie?' I suggested, and quickly moved off on the descent, out of earshot.

Our altitude sickness case had descended by the time we reached the hut, so our publisher escorted us down by the traditional route. He enjoyed the Angel's Dram, but not the Everglades. Back at the car, Davie marvelled at our publisher's sartorial finesse.

'Jist look, he's come through yon swamp and his beets are clean!'

I looked at the footwear in question, with resplendent yellow laces, untouched by mud.

'Ye'd better keep yer ain lacers dubby, Davie, otherwise ye'll be gettin' invited tae jine the S.M.C.'

We stopped, as ever, at Inverarnan for food and a pint. The weather had been glorious here; everyone was in shorts while we were still damp from the Ben. As we were leaving, in came Wee Onie and the Beast. The former I knew: one of the Auld Crowd. He was a gentleman. Always cheery and good crack, a lovely wee man. The other I had heard of from Davie as the epitome of Bad Behaviour, socially and sexually; he looked harmless now, it was difficult to imagine how the tales attached to him could ever have happened. They had been at Stoinaig fishing and had had a fine trip. We told them of ours.

'But I thought ye could only get intae the C.I.C. hut if ye were S.M.C.?' asked Wee Onie innocently.

'We were wi' a couple o' lads fae the S.M.C.,' replied Davie.

There was a silence. Onie looked at the Beast. The Beast looked at Onie.

'Wi' the S.M.C.?' asked the Beast, as if we had said we had been with the Duke of Buccleuch.

There was another silence. Then Wee Onie chirped up: 'come doon some night tae the Scotia bar, Davie, there's a few o' us meet there on a Wednesday. Be glad tae see ye.'

'Fine,' came back Davie, 'it's a wee bit difficult now though, livin oot in Milngavie.'

There was a longer silence, broken by the Beast at last.

'Milngavie?'

'Aye, I flitted jist recently.'

'He's hopin it'll get him intae the S.M.C.,' I joked.

The Beast looked at Onie, who smiled a charming smile. We slapped backs and headed off.

'Maybe,' Davie said in the car, 'saying I'd moved tae Milngavie wis a mistake. It winnae dae my street cred much good wi' yon crowd.'

'Ivvery dream has its price, Davie,' I offered as consolation. 'Ivvery dream has its price.'

COMPLETING: THE END OF AN AULD SANG

I knew he would come anyway. But I also felt I owed him an alibi, for old time's sake. It was my last Munro, Beinn Mheadhoin in the Cairngorms, and a few folk had said they would try and make it to the new Bob Scott's Bothy for the occasion.

'I hope it's no some big horrible lumpy wan?' queried Davie.

'No, it's up past Etchachan, lookin doon on Loch Avon. And there's some nice wee tors on the tap. And I was thinkin . . .'

I paused for effect, and he listened guardedly.

'If we get an early start we could be deen by denner-time, and then it'd be easy tae drap tae Etchachan and dae something on the crag . . .'

I left the seed to germinate. After a while he replied.

'Aye, guid idea. Let's dae Naismith's Route.'

'But there's nae Naismith's route on Etchachan, Davie.'

'There must be, there's a Naismith's Route on ivvery crag,' he insisted. 'But a' right, we'll dae Collie's Climb.'

'But there's nae Collie's Climb either,' I replied, exasperatedly.

'Nae Naismith's Route. Nae Collie's Climb. Whit kind o' a crag is this? But I'd forgotten it wis the Cairngorms. Right, we'll dae Original Route — there must be an Original Route?'

I flicked hurriedly through my old red-covered 1962 Cairngorms Guide Book, and sure enough, there was an Original Route, and only Mild Severe. I showed him the description.

'Disnae sound too bad, but it wis done in 1950! I usually don't touch anything done since 1900 nooadays. Aye, that wid be a guid wye o' completing; finishing aff wi' a wee climb . . .'

We drove up, Davie and I, along with Jack, on a glorious May afternoon, arriving at the Linn o' Dee when the light was sinking. As we packed, we watched the sunlight slanting through the Scots pines by the river, and silvering the blaeberry carpet on the ground. Davie spoke.

128

'I love the Cairngorms. I love the trees, I love the light, I love the space . . .' Then, feeling he might have conceded too much: 'pity aboot the hills, though.'

We humped on packs heavy with climbing gear and celebratory libations, and started up the path. At the roadside were parked dozens of cars. I told Jack, 'in the ten years I went to Scott's fae Aiberdeen, I only wance saw a non-Aberdonian, a wild Lewis teuchter. Noo . . .'

Jack made noises that he thought were appropriate in the context, though I was sure his interest was politely feigned.

At the Black Brig we halted for a rest. I continued my history lesson: after all it was my completion, a certain indulgence from listeners could be expected. Just as I explained that there were not as many fish in the river as formerly, one jumped. Jack pretended not to notice. I began to wonder if the ruined shielings I had promised him were really there, or if senile dementia had played total havoc with my memory. But no, they were there, overrun with rabbits. And I was right about the deer. Hundreds of the stunted beasts, semi-tame now, grazing on the river flats.

'Ye nivver saw a deer doon here in summer, they were a' on the taps. But there cannae be enough for them a' tae eat up there noo. And jist becase some bloody Yank wints his wife tae bide next door tae the Queen, and lets the place ging tae rack and ruin . . . Massacre the buggers.'

'The deer or the lairds?'

'The baith o' them!'

We carried on and watched the light suffuse and dwindle behind Derry Cairngorm and Carn a' Mhaim, still showing much snow. I could see, and pointed out, tomorrow's top. We stopped to look at the Derry Woods. I could smell the resin from the pines and the air rising from the sandy path, so different from the smells of the West Coast.

'Whether that auld bugger Scott is in heaven or hell, he'll be missing the sicht o' the Derry Woods in the gloaming. And the smell,' I added.

We came to a section of the Derry Woods, slaughtered by the landowner for commercial reasons, and descended through the ruined stumps to the bothy. This lay in a lovely haugh by the river, and a half dozen of the pines had been spared around it. We were expecting company, but not exactly the company we found. Erchie Boomer, the Dominie and Rab had come twenty miles over the tops of Beinn Avon and Beinn a' Bhuird to meet us. But there too were another crowd, one of whom I had met before.

And so too, it transpired, had Erchie Boomer met him. We entered, and deposited our sacks, exchanged greetings. Erchie was chatting away to the lad whose brogue confirmed he was from the Granite City. He explained.

'I met Tony here aboot ten year ago, when he was a wee lad. He was on Lochnagar wi' Freddy Malcolm, and I minded his face . . .'

I looked, and minded his face too. About eighteen months before, I had come to the rebuilt Scott's for the first time. We were eight, and Tony was on his own. He was one of the group who had rebuilt the bothy after the fire, and was one of the leaders-off of the 'Winers and Diners', an anarchic crew from Aberdeen. who had just begun to achieve notoriety when I left the city in '73. The group intrigued me for many reasons. They were a throwback, in the days of stripey pants and orange-juice drinking, to the 1960s. Hard drinkers and hard climbers, from the 'Gorms to the Karakorum. Working-class lads (now an endangered species on the hills) working mainly on the rigs, and indulging in bad behaviour when on land. The first time I met Tony, he got quickly drunk, and lay in a semi-coma for nearly twenty-four hours. But this time he was here with his pals, I noticed. Support.

You learn how to deal with things, learn how to pay your dues. These lads had built the place, and allowed unlimited access. They spoke of how every locked hut in Scotland should be sledgehammered open for general use; and how could we, who had broken into locked huts in our own youth, disagree? But they extracted a price for this access — a price which some would not be willing to pay. The price was a barrage of bad behaviour and a torrent of banter. It was clear many could not, and would not wish to, stand their ground.

It started quietly enough. Two of them were slumped unconscious on the bunk.

'They'll be up seen enough,' commented Tony. Threateningly.

Meanwhile Tony and his pal worked their way through a wall of cans of beer, and smoked happily. We were being abstemious, with our great plans for the next day. This drew sarcasm from Tony.

'Aye, you fuckin ageing hippies fae the sixties cannae handle it noo.'

'I did my bad behaviour when I wis young,' came back Davie.

'Aye and that wisni yesterdi, by the look o' ye.'

Erchie assumed the unusual role of mediator.

'I was tellin these lads aboot yer book, Davie and Ian.'

This seemed to produce a split. One lad, older, with a big dog named Wolf, commented, 'I liked it, it was good.'

'Thanks,' I said.

'Fuck, it wis like watchin' pint dry,' said Tony. 'A' thae big words, we's kin jist understand words o' ane syllable.'

'Syllable's got three. Syllables,' I commented.

The banter continued, and we gave as good as we got, till it was time to bed down. Then, convinced they would get a rise out of us, they decided to show us that we would respond to the bait and make their day.

Just as our party stretched out to sleep, the two drugged bodies rose from their bunks, restocked the fire and started to prepare a huge meal. More drink was produced, food cooked and the fire built up till the temperature was like a sauna. It was impossible to sleep, I was pouring sweat. The 'Winers and Diners' were wining and dining. Erchie was seduced, and soon joined them in the drinking and revelries. From the recesses of the doss I heard comments like, 'I dinna ken, Boomer, these are afa folk ye ging aboot wi' noo. Authors and sic like. Folk that ging tae their beds early . . .'

Defend us, Erchie, I thought.

'Weel no, it's jist it's the lad's last Munro the morra, and he'll be wanting a wee sleep.'

And wee sleep we got. At four o'clock their stamina ran out (not the drink, I checked in the morning) and we got about three hours' kip before Wolf woke us all up. We were knackered, but had neither been driven out to sleep under the stars, nor risen to the bait of the bad behaviour. We had paid our dues for the hut.

While we got ready I talked with Wolf's owner. It turned out that not only was he another lad on the dole, living in bothies, but he knew those I had met at Camasunary and at Stavineag, having shared winter accommodation with them over the years. A regular freemasonry of the bothy hobos seems to exist now.

'That's my electric, that's my gas,' he said, pointing to the sun and the fallen timber round the bothy. But I remembered having seen one of the Camasunary crew shivering on a winter street in Glasgow, begging.

We set off up Glen Derry, through the pines. The Dominie was comparing their present positions with those in a set of old Poucher photographs; he is like that, the Dominie. The day was overcast. As we walked someone commented adversely on the behaviour of our bothy-mates. Davie spoke for us both.

'Well, in the first place, I've done exactly that mysel in bothies, so I couldnae complain. And there's a price for everything. I'd rather hae them, wi' their bad behaviour, than yon gear-freaks, day-outers and fitness fanatics that bore ye tae death. They were interesting, and interested. If ye listened, before they got too bad, they spoke o' the ecology, the history, and the total mountain experience. I thought their kind were extinct, but they're nae, and I'm glad o't.'

By now we were pulling up the path to the Etchachan hut, and the mist was lowering onto the tops. As we approached the hut, we came upon a group outside a tent, having a midday breakfast. When they saw our rope, they hastily scrambled their gear together, and headed for the crags. Davie chuckled.

'They're feart we steal their route.'

We lunched as the rain started to fall, lightly. It began to look like we would not get our climb, and might see nothing from our summit. We were all tired after the night, and it was slowly that we ascended the path to Loch Etchachan in the heart of the Cairngorms. There the scene was epic. MacDhui was still covered in snow, and wraiths of mist swirled round the loch, revealing glimpses of the massif beyond. We began the slow toil up Beinn Mheadhoin, speaking little, reaching the first of the granite tors, and seeing the summit far off across the plateau. And some God Unknown had been propitiated by some deed unknown, for a chill north wind got up and cleared the sky of cloud. As we trudged across the plateau, disturbing nesting ptarmigan and dotterel, we could see the Moray Firth beyond the summit, and Bennachie away to the east. To our left the depths of Glen Avon, with the majesty of Hell's Lum Crag and the Shelter Stone Crag, while behind us was MacDhui with the lip of Sputan Dearg smiling at us — or so it seemed.

I scrambled up the summit tor, ahead of the others, and stood in the biting wind. I felt nothing but cold, and took a snifter of the celebratory whisky, handing it to the others as they ascended one by one. A few quick photographs, another swig of whisky, and we were down.

'What will ye dae noo?' asked Erchie.

I thought.

'Well, there's my tops, and the English, Irish and Welsh 3,000 feet hills. Then there's the classic V.Diff's tae complete wi' Davie, and I micht dae a couple of the better Corbetts . . . '

'Speakin o' Corbetts,' said Erchie, 'is that Ben Rinnes?'

He pointed.

'Aye,' I replied, 'and so wis the whisky ye were drinkin. A 1968, tae remind me o' my rebellious youth.'

We started down, lingering to look at the recesses of Loch Avon before stumbling back to Loch Etchachan. It was still cold, and rather later than we had expected to be where we were. I addressed Davie.

'Davie, dae ye think we could safely blame the Winers and Diners for oor failure tae dae Original Route, gin we didnae?'

'Aye, among ither reasons.'

'Forget the ither reasons, that's the official ane.'

I was tired from lack of sleep, but wanted to stay high. The others headed back for the bothy, while Jack and I moved on to Derry Cairngorm, crossing the plateau and getting fine high views into Sputan Dearg. We were dog-tired by the time we were stumbling again through the Derry woods in the gloaming, now less sensitive to their beauty, and just wishing the bothy would appear. We sat a long time outside, feet in the river as the day improved to a fine evening. All ate in silence. We were exhausted, and a lethargy descended on the company. I would rather have slept than celebrated, and indeed had lain down for a wee kip after eating.

But then, rather like Quinn the Eskimo in Dylan's song, Mac arrived. Or rather materialised carrying a guitar, cursing, swearing and blethering.

'Sorry I couldnae mak the hill. Bit ye'll hae got it daen?'

'Aye, gled ye could come.'

Introductions, cups of tea, drams, got the social adrenalin going again, and then someone mentioned that the day before had been Dylan's 50th birthday — that was a cue to Mac. By the time he had worked through "Tambourine Man", "Masters of War" and a few others, our alcohol consumption was rivalling that of the Winers and Diners (who had departed that morning). So boisterous did it become that a couple of ladies from Somerset, who had walked through the Lairig, went outside and sat by the river. Possibly they feared for their honour amongst half a dozen drunken Scotsmen. But the quality of the music was so high that they came back and sat silently on the bunk, watching the proceedings.

> 'Wi' merry sangs an' friendly cracks,
> I wat they didna weary
> And unco tales, an' funny jokes
> Their sports were cheep and cheery.' (Burns, *Halloween*)

'It's a' right,' someone said. 'Ye're quite safe, we've been neutered. Wid ye like a drink, ladies?'

That they refused, and as the hours went by we forgot about them. Mac gave us a medley of classic ballads, holding the audience spellbound with "Harlaw". Jack gave us all his ageing groover's numbers from the Beatles era when his fingers hit the strings, and Erchie sang those ones about miners and bar-room mountaineers. Rab gave us a beautiful rendition of a Burns ballad, and even the Dominie did his bit with a Gaelic song.

'Davie, ye're the only ane that's nae sung for me.'

'I wouldnae want tae spile yer night. And ye seem tae be enjoyin yersel. I can tell by the amount o' bobbin aboot and bad singin yer daein. And drink yer spillin.'

Erchie flaked out first, leaning over a chair in praying posture. Maybe he was worried after all the anti-clerical comments he had made about what we would see on our way to the Pyrenees in summer, and was asking forgiveness.

'On the train tae Lourdes, ye'll be the only wans wi' fower limbs and two eyes. Lock yersel in the guard's van and get drunk, it's the only wye. And they sell widden Jesuses wi' nae arms. If ye want a praying wan, they stick praying airms in, if ye want upraised airms, they stick them into the holes . . .'

Then the Dominie, after an altercation with the fireplace which he lost, staggered outside to spend the night under the stars. Finally Mac, the last man in the world that can sing in the classical ballad style, gave us "Inverey" amidst a deafening silence bar his voice.

> 'Inverey cam' doon Deeside, whistlin and playin,
> He was at bold Brackley's yetts afore day was dawnin.
> Cries Bold Baron Brackley, are ye within?
> There's sharp swords and daggers will gar yer bleed spin.'

'Ye'll nivver hear the like again,' I told the silent room.

'Aye,' said Mac, 'it's like yon Dylan song. I'm a walking antique.'

'Are we nae a', Mac? Are we nae a'?'

And he gave me the "Gallowa' Hills" as a lullaby.

In the morning we were sprawled about the floor in various postures of discomfort and with varying degrees of after-effect. I heard the ladies from Somerset prepare to depart, and wished they would not make so much noise. They took their packs outside, and then, rather formally, re-entered the bothy.

135

'We'd just like to say one thing,' announced the elder of the two.

Oh, no, I thought. Unpleasantness. I tried to creep under the bunk and out of the way, hoping they would blame Erchie who was nearest the door.

'Thank you for the music. That was a wonderful night. We'll never forget it.'

Silence. No one answered. Then I said, hesitantly, 'I thought we might hae been keepin ye awake?'

'We can sleep anytime. That experience was worth staying awake for.'

'Well, it's a lang time since a woman's said that tae me, but thanks a' the same,' I answered, though I could hardly claim credit for the music.

They departed and we made slower preparations to do likewise. A long hungover breakfast, a slow fester by the river in the sunshine, and after a few hours everyone was ready to go. Everyone bar me. I still had a little headache, which I put down to sinusitis.

'Na, na,' said Erchie, 'it's mixing watter wi' yer drink, I saw ye last night. Hae a wee snifter and ye'll feel better.'

I declined, leaving Erchie to finish a half-bottle between the bothy and the Linn.

They went, leaving me to snooze, then — recovered — to stroll past Luibeg and kick through the ashes of the old bothy where I had spent so many nights so many years ago. It was an evening of faery, the sun casting long shadows from the pines which were full of chattering birds. The sun glistened on the peaks, turning the snow pink. I thought of what Mac had said. Walking Antiques. The teams that still sang in the bothies. That had the old gear and still cooked by primus. That sometimes felt like Indians on a reservation in the new order of things. I myself had a reservation about Davie's optimism over the Winers and Diners: they could not sing. But maybe they would learn, or recruit a singer? And carry on the fight against cultural entropy.

Back home Davie commented, 'that was a night o' quality. Ye should be honoured, honoured. It's almost worth completing yer Munros for.'

'Weel, let's dae a deal. I'll come wi' ye on three boring Munros for ivvery classic V.Diff ye haul me up — hoo's that?'

I am still awaiting an answer. But there is time yet. Plenty of time. I know Davie well enough now to know that.